The Silver Burdett
Mathematical
Dictionary

The Silver Burdett
Mathematical
Dictionary

R.E. Jason Abdelnoor

Head of Mathematics Department,
Slatyford School, Newcastle upon Tyne

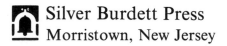 Silver Burdett Press
Morristown, New Jersey

The photograph of the highway on page 54
is reproduced by courtesy of Aerofilms Ltd

First published 1979
A. Wheaton & Company Limited
A Division of Pergamon Press

Adapted and published in the United States
in 1987 by Silver Burdett Press,
Morristown, New Jersey

Library of Congress Cataloging in Publication Data

Abdelnoor, R. E. Jason.
   Silver Burdett mathematical dictionary.

   Summary: A dictionary of mathematical terms
from abacus to zero, with illustrations, diagrams,
and cross-references.
   1. Mathematics — Dictionaries, Juvenile.
[1. Mathematics — Dictionaries]   I. Title.
II. Title: Mathematical dictionary.
QA5.A23   1987   510′.3′21   86-45568
ISBN 0-382-09309-7
ISBN 0-382-09485-9 (Hardcover)
ISBN: 84-599-1981-1 (Rústica)
ISBN: 84-599-1985-4 (Cartoné)
Depósito legal: M. 17.970-1987
Imprime: Edime, Organización Gráfica, S. A.
Polígono Industrial de Arroyomolinos, Calle D, 14
Móstoles (Madrid)
Impreso en España - Printed in Spain

Introduction

Mathematics is a language. Therefore people cannot think mathematically, nor express themselves in mathematical terms unless they have first learned the correct meaning of the words that are available to use.

In recent years, with the development of modern mathematics, the scope of the subject has broadened considerably. Consequently, the variety of words and concepts has increased. The function of this dictionary is to explain the mathematical terms now appearing in mathematics books and courses, covering the teaching ranges from the ages 11 to 18. It is a handy reference tool for the classroom, the library, and the home.

How to use this book

The mathematical terms are set out alphabetically as in a general dictionary. To understand one mathematical term, it is often necessary to comprehend others with which it is linked. Cross-references to other terms that appear as separate entries are indicated by means of italic type. For example, in the sample given below, the italicized word *quadrilateral* is defined in this dictionary.

To emphasize a particular feature in a diagram or an explanation, various words, lines, or figures are printed in red, as shown in the following sample.

Sample

Rhombus

A rhombus is a *quadrilateral* formed with four equal sides.

Examples:

In general a rhombus has:
- two *lines of symmetry* (its *diagonals*);
- *rotational symmetry* of *order* 2;
- opposite sides *parallel*;
- opposite *angles* equal;
- diagonals *bisecting* each other at *right angles*:
- diagonals bisecting the angles of the rhombus.

5

Abacus (plural Abaci)

An abacus is a device used for counting.
Examples: The upper three abaci are used for counting in the *base* ten number system.

child's
abacus

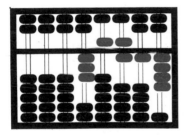

Chinese
abacus showing
the numbers
00035614

Japanese abacus
showing the
numbers
00124589

This spike abacus
can be used for
counting in
base five.

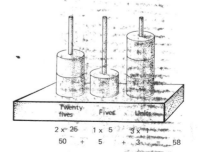

Twenty-fives	Fives	Units	
2 x 25	1 x 5	3 x 1	
50	+ 5	+ 3	= 58

Acceleration

The acceleration of a body is the change in *speed* per unit of time.

Examples: A car is accelerating uniformly along a straight road, and its speed (meters per second) is recorded every 5 seconds, as shown in this table:

speed, m/s	6	12	18	24	30
time, s	0	5	10	15	20

The constant acceleration over this period is

$$\frac{6 \text{ m/s}}{5 \text{ s}} = 1.2 \text{ m/s}^2$$

A sprinter in the Olympic Games reaches a speed of 36 km/h in the first 4 seconds of his race. His average acceleration over the first 4 seconds is

$$\frac{36 \text{ km/h}}{4 \text{ s}} = \frac{36{,}000 \text{ m/h}}{4 \text{ s}}$$

$$= \frac{36{,}000 \text{ m/s}}{60 \times 60 \times 4 \text{ s}}$$

$$= 2.5 \text{ m/s}^2$$

Acute

Acute means sharp. An acute *angle* is a sharply pointed angle whose size is between 0° and 90°.

Examples:

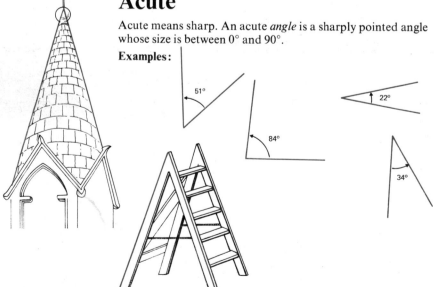

Additive inverse

The additive inverse is the *inverse* under addition. It is the number which, when added to the given number, gives the *identity element* for addition.

Examples:
The additive inverse of 3 is ⁻3, because $3 + {}^-3 = 0$
The additive inverse of 5 is ⁻5, because $5 + {}^-5 = 0$
The additive inverse of ⁻6 is 6, because ${}^-6 + 6 = 0$
The additive inverse of $-\frac{1}{2}$ is $\frac{1}{2}$, because ${}^-\frac{1}{2} + \frac{1}{2} = 0$

NOTE: 0 is the identity for addition of numbers.

With *vectors* and *matrices* (shown below) similar rules apply.

The additive inverse of $\begin{pmatrix} 3 \\ -5 \end{pmatrix}$ is $\begin{pmatrix} {}^-3 \\ 5 \end{pmatrix}$, because

$$\begin{pmatrix} 3 \\ -5 \end{pmatrix} + \begin{pmatrix} {}^-3 \\ 5 \end{pmatrix} = \begin{pmatrix} 0 \\ 0 \end{pmatrix}$$

The additive inverse of $\begin{pmatrix} 1 & 0 \\ -2 & 4 \end{pmatrix}$ is $\begin{pmatrix} {}^-1 & 0 \\ 2 & {}^-4 \end{pmatrix}$, because

$$\begin{pmatrix} 1 & 0 \\ -2 & 4 \end{pmatrix} + \begin{pmatrix} {}^-1 & 0 \\ 2 & {}^-4 \end{pmatrix} = \begin{pmatrix} 0 & 0 \\ 0 & 0 \end{pmatrix}$$

See **Vector**

Affine transformations

Transformations, which always *map parallel* lines onto parallel lines are called affine transformations.

Examples: *Shears* and *stretches* are affine transformations. Parallelism is *invariant* under these transformations.

The *similarities* are a *subset* of the affine transformations.

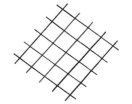

Examples: *Translations*, *reflections*, and *enlargements* are affine transformations.

All affine transformations of the *plane* can be represented by the *matrix* form

$$\begin{pmatrix} x' \\ y' \end{pmatrix} = \begin{pmatrix} a & b \\ c & d \end{pmatrix}\begin{pmatrix} x \\ y \end{pmatrix} + \begin{pmatrix} h \\ k \end{pmatrix}$$

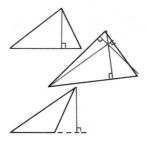

Altitude of a triangle

An altitude is the line from a *vertex* of a *triangle* drawn *perpendicular* to the side opposite the vertex.

Examples (left): Some of the possible altitudes are shown in red.

An altitude may be inside or outside the triangle. There are three altitudes for each triangle, one from each vertex, and they all pass through the same point.

Angle

Angle between rays

small angle An angle is the amount of turn from one *ray* to another.

Examples: When any two straight lines meet at a point, they form an angle. The point where the lines meet is called a *vertex*.

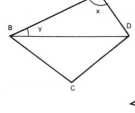

large angle

vertex

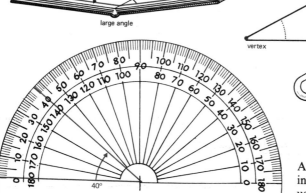

Angles are measured in degrees. A protractor is used to measure angles.

40°

Angles of a polygon

The angles of a *polygon* are the angles between the sides.

Examples: In the figure ABCD we can refer to angle x as ∠A; but for angle y we must refer to it as ∠ABD, not ∠B, to avoid ambiguity.

The angles of the two polygons below are shown in red.

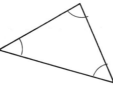

Direction of angles
Clockwise (left): this is the direction in which the hands on a clock turn.
Counter-clockwise: this is the opposite direction.

Bearings are measured clockwise.

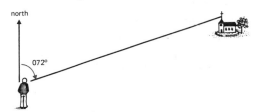

Rotations are called *positive* when they are counter-clockwise.

Angle bisector see Bisector

Angle of depression see Depression

Angle of elevation see Elevation

Apex see Pyramid

Arc

An arc is part of a circle.
An arc is a line, straight or curved, which joins two points.

Example (left):
The red part is an arc of the circle.

In a *network* an arc joins two *nodes* A and B.

Example (left):
There are six arcs in this network: p, q, r, s, t, and u.
There are three arcs between *nodes* A and B.

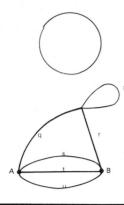

Area

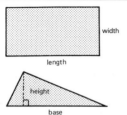

The area is the number of square units of a surface. The surface may be *plane* (flat) or curved, as the surface of a ball.
Here are ways of finding areas of important shapes:

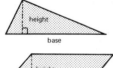

area of *rectangle* = length × width

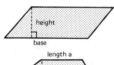

area of *triangle* = $\frac{1}{2}$ × base × height

area of *parallelogram* = base × height

area of *trapezoid* = $\frac{1}{2}$ × (a + b) × height

Arithmetic mean

The arithmetic mean is what most people call the 'average.'
See **Mean**

Arrow diagrams

Arrow diagrams show a *relation* between *sets* of things, such as people or numbers. See **Correspondence, Transpose.**
Examples:

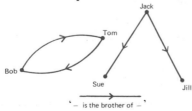

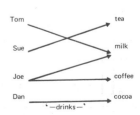

Associative

An *operation* (∗) is said to be associative if it does not matter where parentheses are placed when three *elements* are combined.

(a∗b)∗c = a∗(b∗c) is true if ∗ is associative.

Examples:

numbers under $\begin{cases} \text{addition and} \\ \text{multiplication} \end{cases}$ ARE associative

$(2 + 3) + 5 = 2 + (3 + 5)$
$(4 \times 2) \times 3 = 4 \times (2 \times 3)$

numbers under $\begin{cases} \textit{subtraction} \text{ and} \\ \textit{division} \end{cases}$ are NOT associative

$(4 - 3) - 1 \neq 4 - (3 - 1)$
$(12 \div 6) \div 2 \neq 12 \div (6 \div 2)$

matrices under $\begin{cases} \text{addition} \\ \text{multiplication} \end{cases}$ ARE associative.

Average

A teacher might ask for an average member of the class to represent the class at chess or football. An average is one member or one value that represents the whole group. Mathematicians use three very important averages: *mean*, *median*, and *mode*.

Axis (plural Axes)

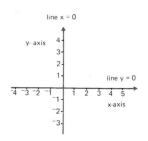

line x = 0
y- axis
line y = 0
x-axis

Axes are the reference lines on a *graph*. On a *coordinate* graph, the line going across has the x numbers and so is called the x-axis. The line going up the page has the y numbers and so is called the y-axis. The point where the lines cross is called the *origin* and represents *zero* on both axes.

NOTE: The *equation* of the x-axis is y = 0 because the y-coordinate is 0 for every point on it. Similarly the y-axis has equation x = 0.

Bar graph

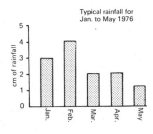

Typical rainfall for Jan. to May 1976
cm of rainfall

Bar graphs show information in a *graphical* form by the use of columns or bars. The length or height of the columns or bars corresponds to the size it represents. Rainfall is often shown by means of a bar graph.

Example (left):

13

Base

The base of a number is the size of the group used.
When counting things, we use groups.

Example (left): There are 2 groups of five sheep and 3 sheep
on their own. So the number of sheep is here represented as 23_{five}.
The diagram shows counting in base five. The number of sheep
is 23_{five}.

Examples: Our normal counting number system is called base ten
because the group size used is ten.
We use ten *digits*, 0, 1, 2, 3, 4, 5, 6, 7, 8, 9.
The place values are *multiples* of ten so that
the 6 in 7614 stands for 6×100,
the 6 in 8563 stands for 6×10,
352 stands for $(3 \times 100) + (5 \times 10) + (2 \times 1)$.

We can count in other bases, such as base 6, using the digits
0, 1, 2, 3, 4, 5.
The group sizes are 6, $6 \times 6 (=36)$, $6 \times 6 \times 6 (= 216)$
so that 3425 stands for

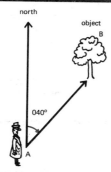

$$(3 \times 216) + (4 \times 36) + (2 \times 6) + (5 \times 1) = 648 + 144 + 12 + 5$$
$$\text{(in base ten)}$$
$$= 809_{ten}$$

Bearing

The bearing of an object is the *angle* measured *clockwise* from
north to the object.
Bearings always have three *digits*. $040°$, NOT JUST $40°$.

Examples:

bearing of B
from A is
$040°$

bearing of C
from D is
$230°$

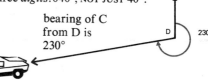

Binary numbers

Binary means two, so binary numbers are numbers in *base* two.
In the binary system only two *digits* are used: 0 and 1. The place
values are

			32	16	8	4	2	1
					1	0	1_{two}	$= 5_{ten}$
				1	1	0	0_{two}	$= 12_{ten}$
			1	1	0	1	1_{two}	$= 27_{ten}$

Binary operation   see **Operation**

Bisector

A bisector cuts something into two equal parts.

Examples:

- A line which cuts an *angle* into two equal parts is called an angle bisector.
- One line is a bisector of another line if it cuts it into two equal parts.

  Line p is a bisector of line AB.

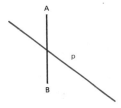

If the bisector of AB is also at *right angles* to AB, the bisector is called the *perpendicular* bisector of AB. This line is sometimes called the *mediator* of AB.

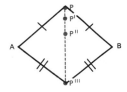

NOTE: The mediator of AB is the *locus* of points P, which are equidistant from A and B.

Boundary

The boundary of a figure is the line around the outside of the figure. The length of the boundary is called the *perimeter*.

Example: The boundaries are shown in red.

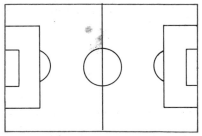

soccer field

15

Cancel

Cancelling a *fraction* is finding an *equivalent fraction* with smaller numbers. See **Equivalent fractions**.

Examples:

$\frac{12}{15} = \frac{3 \times 4}{3 \times 5}$ which cancels to $\frac{4}{5}$

$\frac{14}{21} = \frac{7 \times 2}{7 \times 3}$ which cancels to $\frac{2}{3}$

$\frac{24}{32} = \frac{8 \times 3}{8 \times 4}$ which cancels to $\frac{3}{4}$.

Center of rotation

The center of rotation is the one point which does not move when you do a *rotation*. Where tracing paper is used, the center of rotation is the point where you put your pen or compass point.

Examples:

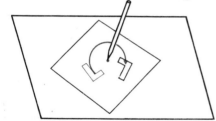

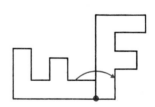

The centers of rotation are shown in red.

Centimeter

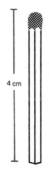

A centimeter is one-hundredth of a *meter*.
1 cm $= \frac{1}{100}$ m and is this long ⌞_____⌟.
                                                   1 cm

NOTE: We shorten centimeter to cm.

Examples:

This matchstick
is 4 cm long.

4 cm

This line is 5 cm in length.

Chord

A line joining two points of a *circle* is called a chord.

Examples:

These lines show just SOME of the chords of this circle.

A chord that passes through the center of the circle is called a *diameter*.

There is only ONE diameter through A.

Circle

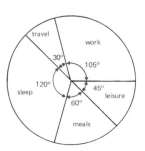

A circle is the *set* of all points in a *plane* at a fixed distance, the *radius*, from a fixed point, the center.

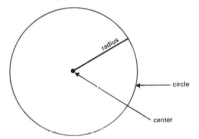

Example (left): The *locus* of a weight being swung on the end of a piece of string is a circle.

For the *area* inside a circle, see **Pi**.
See also **Arc, Circumference, Sector of a circle, Segment of a circle, Semicircle**

Circle graph

A circle graph is a way of representing information.

Example (left):
This circle graph shows how Jimmy Smith spent last Saturday.
15 degrees represents 1 hour.

NOTE: The *circle* is divided into *sectors* so that the *areas* of the *sectors* represent the *data*.

Circumference

The circumference of a *circle* is the distance around the circle.
It is a special name for the *perimeter* of a circle.
The circumference is roughly 3 times the *diameter* (d).
Circumference $= \pi \times diameter$
For π see **Pi.**

Example (left): The circumference of this circle is approximately
$3 \times 4 = 12$ cm.

The circumference of a circle is also the distance rolled by
a circle before coming the same way again.

The circumference of the dime is shown by the length of the
red line.

Clockwise see **Angles**

Closed set

A *set* under the *operation* ∗ is closed when any two *elements* of
the set combine to give another element of the set.

Examples:

$$\left\{ \begin{pmatrix} 1 & 0 \\ 0 & 1 \end{pmatrix}, \begin{pmatrix} ^-1 & 0 \\ 0 & 1 \end{pmatrix}, \begin{pmatrix} 1 & 0 \\ 0 & ^-1 \end{pmatrix}, \begin{pmatrix} ^-1 & 0 \\ 0 & ^-1 \end{pmatrix} \right\}$$

Under multiplication the set is closed, because the *product* of any
two *members* of the set is in the set.

$\{1, 2, 3, 4, 5, 6, 7, 8\}$ Under addition the set is NOT closed because,
for example, $4 + 5 = 9$ and 9 is NOT in the set.

However, $\{0, 1, 2, 3, 4\}$ under "clock" addition the set is closed,
as can be seen from this table.

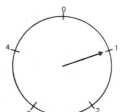

⊕	0	1	2	3	4
0	0	1	2	3	4
1	1	2	3	4	0
2	2	3	4	0	1
3	3	4	0	1	2
4	4	0	1	2	3

Coefficient

In a mathematical *expression* the coefficients are the numbers of each *variable*.

Example: In $5x + 3y$, 5 is the coefficient of x, and 3 is the coefficient of y.

Column

A list of numbers (or letters) going down the page is called a column.
Vectors are often written as a column.

Examples:

$$\begin{pmatrix} 2 \\ -3 \end{pmatrix} \qquad \begin{pmatrix} 1 \\ 4 \\ 0 \\ 5 \end{pmatrix} \qquad \begin{pmatrix} 2 \\ 0 \\ 1 \\ 7 \end{pmatrix}$$

When a *matrix* consists only of a column, it is called a column matrix.

Commutative

An *operation* on a *set* is commutative when it does not matter in which order the elements are combined. The operation $*$ on a set is commutative if

$$a*b = b*a$$

for all *members* of the set.

Examples:

Addition of numbers IS commutative, and $\qquad\qquad 3+5=5+3$

multiplication of numbers IS commutative, $\qquad 7 \times 2 = 2 \times 7$
But
division of numbers is NOT commutative, and $\qquad 3 \div 6 \neq 6 \div 3$

subtraction of numbers is NOT commutative. $\qquad 4 - 2 \neq 2 - 4$

Addition of *matrices* IS commutative.

$$\begin{pmatrix} 0 & 1 \\ 2 & 3 \end{pmatrix} + \begin{pmatrix} 4 & 7 \\ 0 & 1 \end{pmatrix} = \begin{pmatrix} 4 & 7 \\ 0 & 1 \end{pmatrix} + \begin{pmatrix} 0 & 1 \\ 2 & 3 \end{pmatrix}$$

but multiplication of matrices is NOT commutative.

$$\begin{pmatrix} 1 & -1 \\ 2 & 1 \end{pmatrix}\begin{pmatrix} 3 & 0 \\ 1 & -1 \end{pmatrix} \neq \begin{pmatrix} 3 & 0 \\ 1 & -1 \end{pmatrix}\begin{pmatrix} 1 & -1 \\ 2 & 1 \end{pmatrix}$$

19

Complement of a set

The complement of a *set* A in $\mathscr{E}$ is the set of all *elements of $\mathscr{E}$* NOT in A, and is shown by the *symbol* A'.

$\mathscr{E}$ **Example (left):**

If $\mathscr{E} = \{1, 2, 3, 4, 5, 6, 7, 8, 9\}$
and A is the *{odd numbers}* $= \{1, 3, 5, 7, 9\}$
then A' is the *{even numbers}* $= \{2, 4, 6, 8\}$

The complement of A is the region shaded red.

NOTE: A *union* A' is the *universal set* $A \cup A' = \mathscr{E}$

Complementary angles

If two *angles* such as 63° and 27° add up to 90°, they are called complementary angles. One angle is said to be the complement of the other.

$27° + 63° = 90°$

Concave polygons

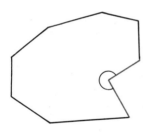

A *polygon* which is not *convex* is said to be concave.

Examples:

The concave part is shown in red.

In a concave polygon, one or more of its *angles* is more than 180°.

Cone

A cone is a solid which usually has a circular base and tapers to a point at the top, called its *vertex*.

Examples:

The *area* of the curved surface of a cone is given by
curved area = $\pi \times$ *radius* $\times$ *slant height.*
$$A = \pi r l$$

The *volume* of a come is given by
volume = $\frac{1}{3} \times$ base area $\times$ height.
$$V = \frac{1}{3}\pi r^2 h$$

Congruent

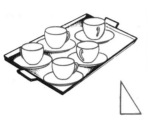

If two objects have the same shape and size, they are congruent.

Examples: Each cup and saucer (**left**) is congruent to every other cup and saucer.

△ and △ ARE congruent shapes.

◠ and ◡ ARE congruent shapes.

▢ and ▫ are not the same size and so they are NOT congruent.

▭ and ▱ are not the same shape and so they are NOT congruent.

If congruent shapes have the same *sense*, they are directly congruent; if they are congruent but there is a change in sense, they are oppositely congruent.

Constant

A constant is a fixed number. Its value does not change.

Pi (π) has a constant value of 3.1416...

Continuous quantity

How much do these apples weigh?

Weight is a continuous quantity because the answer can be ANY value: 2.1841...kg
   or 2.1842...kg
   or 10.700701...kg

The spring scale measures a change in weight continuously.
A platform balance, using individual weights, can measure only changes equal to the smallest weight.

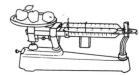

Other continuous quantities are length, *area*, height, *volume*, temperature and *speed*. As a car *accelerates* from start to 50 miles per hour, the speed must pass through ALL values between 0 and 50.

Quantities which are NOT continuous are called *discrete*.

NOTE: When x is continuous, we use ALL the points on the number line.

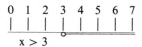

x > 3

Convex polygons

These *polygons* are called convex because all their *vertices* point outward.

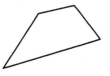

A shape is convex if the line joining ANY two points on the shape stays inside the shape.

Shapes which are NOT convex are called *concave*.

Coordinates

A point on a *graph* can be fixed by a pair of numbers which describe its position with reference to the x and y *axes*.

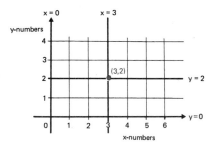

Example: The point where the lines x = 3 and y = 2 cross is labeled (3, 2).

The coordinates of the point are 3 and 2.

The first number, 3, is called the x-coordinate.

The second number, 2, is called the y-coordinate.

NOTE: (2, 3) is NOT the same point as (3, 2). See **Ordered pairs**.

Correspondence

Types of relations are called correspondences.
Arrow diagrams are classified into four types of
correspondences.

Examples:

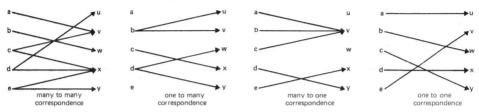

many to many correspondence	one to many correspondence	many to one correspondence	one to one correspondence

These *relations* are NOT *mappings*.　　　These relations ARE mappings.

Corresponding points

Points are said to be corresponding when, under *transformations*
such as *enlargement*, *rotation*, *reflection*, *translation*, etc., one point
is the *object* and the other is its *image*.

Examples:

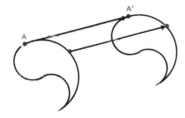 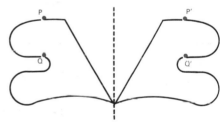

A and A′⎫
P and P′⎬ are corresponding points.
Q and Q′⎭

Cosine

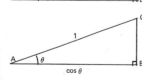

The cosine of *angle* θ is written as cos θ.

Cosine of angles less than 90°

$$\cos \theta = \frac{AB}{AC} \qquad \cos \theta = \frac{\text{adjacent side}}{\text{hypotenuse}}$$

When the length of AC is 1,
$$\cos \theta = AB$$

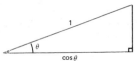

When this triangle is *enlarged*, by *scale factor* r,
$$PQ = r \cos \theta$$

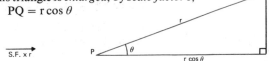

Examples:

$\cos x = \frac{4}{5}$
$\cos x = 0.8$
$\cos 36.9° = 0.800$ (from tables)
$x = 36.9°$

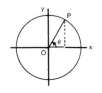

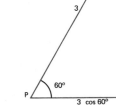

$$PQ = \cos 60°$$
$$= 3 \times 0.5 \qquad (\cos 60° = 0.5 \text{ from tables})$$
$$= 1.5$$

Cosine of any angle

If a line OP of unit length turns through an angle θ from the x-*axis*, the cosine of θ is the x-*coordinate* of P shown in red.

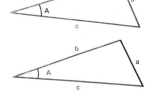

Cosine rule

When the lengths of the sides of a *triangle* are known, angle A can be found by the rule

$$\cos A = \frac{b^2 + c^2 - a^2}{2bc}$$

When an angle and the two sides which form the angle are known, the third side can be found using the rule in this form

$$a^2 = b^2 + c^2 - 2bc \cos A$$

Counting numbers

Counting numbers are the numbers people first used to count things like sheep.

The set of counting numbers is $\{1, 2, 3, 4, 5, 6, 7, 8, \ldots\}$

The set of counting numbers is the same as the set of *natural numbers* and is a *subset* of the *integers*.

Cube

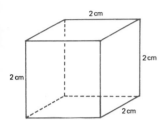

A cube is a *regular* solid with all its *faces square* and all its edges equal in length. The shape of a die is a cube.

This is a diagram of a 2 cm cube.

Examples:

Cubed

A number cubed is the number to the *power* 3.

Example: 2 cubed is $2^3 = 8$

Cubic centimeter

A cubic centimeter is a *unit* for measuring *volume*. Cubic centimeter is shortened to cm^3.

One cubic centimeter is the same volume as a *cube* whose edges are one *centimeter*.

Example: The volume of this *rectangular prism* is
$$2 \times 3 \times 7 = 42\,\text{cm}^3.$$

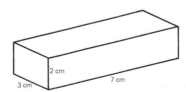

25

Cubic meter

A cubic meter is the standard unit for measuring *volume*. Cubic meter is shortened to m³.

One cubic meter is the same volume as a *cube* whose edges are one *meter* in length.

Example: The volume of this *rectangular prism* is $\frac{1}{2} \times \frac{1}{2} \times 20 = 5$ m³.

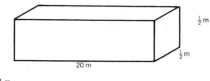

NOTE: 1 m³ $= 100 \times 100 \times 10$ cm³
1 m³ $= 1,000,000$ cm³

Cuboid

A cuboid (usually called a rectangular prism) is a solid that has *rectangles* for all of its *faces*.

See **Rectangular prism**

Examples:

Cumulative frequency

The cumulative frequency is the *sum* of the *frequencies* at or below a given value.

Example: In a survey, 100 children were asked what size shoe they wore.

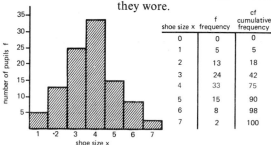

shoe size x	f frequency	cf cumulative frequency
0	0	0
1	5	5
2	13	18
3	24	42
4	33	75
5	15	90
6	8	98
7	2	100

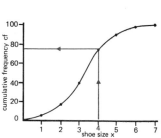

The frequency of shoe size 4 is 33, but there are 75 children with a shoe size of 4 or less. 75 is the cumulative frequency of size 4.

Cylinder

A cylinder is a space figure with two parallel bases that are congruent circles.

Examples:

The surface area of the curved part of the cylinder is given by:
circumference (πD) × height

$A = \pi D \times h$

The space figure at the left can be opened into the plane figure at the right.

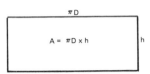

$$A = \pi D \times h$$

The *volume* of the cylinder is given by:
Volume = area of end × height

$V = A \times h$
$V = \pi r^2 h$

Data

Data are numbers which have been collected for study. Data can be displayed by *bar graphs*, *circle graphs*, *pictograms*, etc.

Examples: A class of 23 pupils are asked how many children there are in each of their families. The following data are collected:
2, 1, 1, 2, 3, 3, 1, 2, 1, 4, 1, 2, 2, 3, 3, 3, 6, 4, 2, 3, 2, 2, 3.

There are five families with 1 child, eight families with 2 children, seven families with 3 children, two families with 4 children, and just one family with 6 children.

Decagon

A decagon is a *polygon* with ten straight sides and ten *angles.*

Examples:

This is a *regular* decagon.

Decimal fraction

A *fraction* with a *denominator* of 10, or 100, or 1,000, or 10,000...
is a decimal fraction.

Examples:

$$\frac{3}{10}, \quad \frac{17}{100}, \quad \frac{20}{100}, \quad \frac{427}{10,000}$$

NOTE: They can be easily put into decimals.

$$\frac{3}{10} = 0.3, \quad \frac{17}{100} = 0.17, \quad \frac{20}{100} = 0.20, \quad \frac{427}{10,000} = 0.0427$$

Decimal point

A dot is used to separate *whole numbers* and their parts when
writing a number using place notation. The dot is called a decimal
point.

Examples: $17\frac{9}{10}$ is written 17.9.
$2\frac{3}{5}$ could be written 2.6.
$3\frac{1}{4}$ could be written 3.25.

Denominator see **Fraction**

Depression

The *angle* of depression is the angle measured DOWNWARDS from
the *horizontal* to an object.

Example:

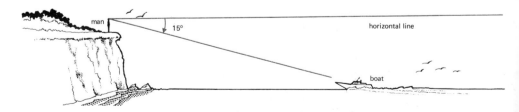

The angle of depression of the boat from the man is 15°.

Determinant

The determinant of a *matrix*, **M**, is a special number that goes with matrix, **M**. It can be found like this:

when $\mathbf{M} = \begin{pmatrix} a & b \\ c & d \end{pmatrix}$

then the determinant of **M** is $ad - bc$.

The determinant of matrix **M** is shortened to $|\mathbf{M}|$ or det **M**.

Example:

$$\det \begin{pmatrix} 3 & 5 \\ 2 & 4 \end{pmatrix} = \begin{vmatrix} 3 & 5 \\ 2 & 4 \end{vmatrix}$$
$$= 3 \times 4 - 2 \times 5$$
$$= 2.$$

When the matrix is used to represent a *transformation*, its determinant is the area *scale factor* of the transformation.

Diagonal

A diagonal is a straight line drawn from one *vertex* of a *polygon* or a *polyhedron* to another vertex.

Examples:
Diagonal of a polygon

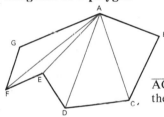

All the diagonals are shown on this figure.

$\overline{AC}$, $\overline{AD}$, $\overline{AE}$ and $\overline{AF}$ are ALL the diagonals from A.

Diagonal of a polyhedron

The one and only diagonal from the vertex H is shown by the red line $\overline{HK}$.

Diameter

A diameter of a *circle* is any line that joins two points of the circle and passes through the center.

Examples:

All the diameters of a circle are the same length. They are twice the *radius*.

Difference

The difference of two numbers is the quantity when the smaller number, the **minuend** is *subtracted* from the bigger number, the **subtrahend.**

Examples:

The difference between 8 and 3 is 5. $8 - 3 = 5$
The difference between 3 and 8 is 5. $8 - 3 = 5$.
Remainder is the same as difference.

Digit

A digit is any single figure used when representing a number. In our *base* ten number system, which we use daily, the digits are 0, 1, 2, 3, 4, 5, 6, 7, 8, 9.

Example: The digits used in 107,585 are 0, 1, 5, 7, 8.

Direct route

In a *network* of *nodes* and *arcs* a direct route between two nodes is a route that does NOT go through another node.

Example:

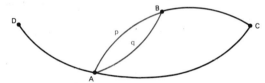

There are two direct routes, p and q, between the nodes A and B.
There is NO DIRECT route from D to B.

See **Route matrix**

Discrete quantity

When we ask the question "How many?" we are looking at a discrete quantity. The answer must be exact, and we usually use the *counting numbers.*

Examples: How many cars are there? The answer must be exact, and in this case it must be a *whole number.*

How much money have I in my pocket? The answer must be exact, but in this case we count in dollars and cents. The answer may be $2.32, $5.45, $6.50, $10.70 but NOT $10.70321.

NOTE: When x is discrete, we use only SOME of the points on the number line. For example, x > 3 is shown by

Quantities which are NOT discrete are called *continuous*.

Displacement

A displacement (or *journey*) is a change in position. The displacement is defined by giving both the distance and the direction.

Example:

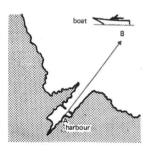

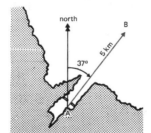

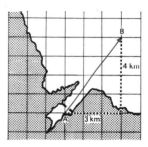

The dispacement from harbor A to boat B is represented by the red line and can be defined
either as 5 km, *bearing* 037°
or as 3 km east, 4 km north.
Displacement is a *vector* quantity, and so it can be best described using a vector.

Example: For the displacement harbor to boat, shown above,

$$AB = \begin{pmatrix} 3 \\ 4 \end{pmatrix}$$

Distributive

When for a *set* of *elements* {a, b, c, d,...} there are two binary operations such as × and +, then × is distributive over +. Multiplication is said to have a distributive property over addition.

Examples:
a) With numbers × is distributive over +
   3 × (4 + 5) = (3 × 4) + (3 × 5)
b) With sets ∩ is distributive over ∪
   A ∩ (B ∪ C) = (A ∩ B) ∪ (A ∩ C)

Dividend

In a division the dividend is the number being divided.

Example:

In the division $\dfrac{5203}{4)20{,}812}$ 20,812 is the dividend

---

Divisor

In a division the divisor is the number you are dividing by.

Example:

In the division $\dfrac{2014}{3)6{,}042}$ the divisor is 3

Dodecagon

A *polygon* bounded by twelve straight lines and containing twelve *angles* is a dodecagon.

Examples:

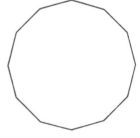

This is a *regular* dodecagon.

Dodecahedron

A dodecahedron is a solid shape with twelve *faces*. All the faces of a *regular* dodecahedron are regular *pentagons*.

Example: This is a regular dodecahedron.

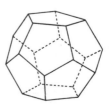

Domain

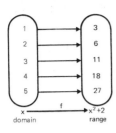

x ———f——→ x²+2
domain   range

The domain of a *function* is the *set* of numbers *mapped* by the function.

NOTE: The domain is sometimes called the *object* set.

Example (left): $\{1, 2, 3, 4, 5\}$ is the domain.

See **Range**

Duodecimal

$$t_{twelve} = 10_{ten}$$
$$14_{twelve} = 16_{ten}$$
$$18_{twelve} = 20_{ten}$$
$$21_{twelve} = 25_{ten}$$

A duodecimal number is a number written in *base* twelve. If we use the *symbols* t for ten and e for eleven, then the *digits* in base twelve are 0, 1, 2, 3, 4, 5, 6, 7, 8, 9, t, e

Examples (left):

Element

The elements of a *set* are the things in the set.

Examples:
If $A = \{$first 5 letters of the alphabet$\}$, then the elements of A are a, b, c, d, and e.
If $P = \{$prime numbers between 4 and 20$\}$, then the elements of P are 5, 7, 11, 13, 17, and 19.
The number of elements in set A is five, this is written as
$$n(A) = 5$$
Similarly, $n(P) = 6$
Each letter or number in a *matrix* is also called an element.

Elevation

The *angle* of elevation is the angle measured UPWARDS from the *horizontal* to an object.

Example:

The angle of elevation of the kite from the man is 30°.

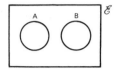

Empty set

When a *set* has no *elements*, it is called the empty set and is shown as {}, or by the *symbol* φ.

Example (left): If A = {6, 8, 10, 12} and B = {1, 3, 5, 7}, then A ∩ B = {} or φ.

Enlargement

Enlargement is a *transformation* which *maps* a shape onto a *similar* shape, from a center O using a *scale factor* k.

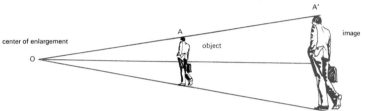

To find the *image*, A′, of a point A of the *object*, a line is drawn from O through A. A′ is then on $\overline{OA}$ and

$$OA' = k \times OA$$

In the example above, the scale factor is 2.

The lines through O, used to draw the image, are called *pattern lines*.

When the scale factor k is a *fraction*, the image is smaller than the object.

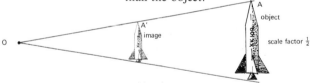

When the scale factor k is *negative*, the enlarged image is also *rotated* 180° about O.

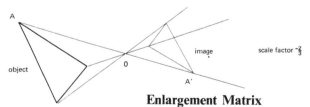

Enlargement Matrix

The *transformation* $\begin{pmatrix} x \\ y \end{pmatrix} \rightarrow \begin{pmatrix} k & 0 \\ 0 & k \end{pmatrix}\begin{pmatrix} x \\ y \end{pmatrix}$ represents an enlargement with center at the *origin*, and scale factor k.

NOTE: This scale factor, k, is the *linear scale factor*. The area scale factor is k^2, the *determinant* of the *matrix*.

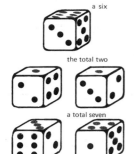

a six

the total two

a total seven

Equally likely outcomes

Outcomes, or events, are equally likely if the chance of them happening is the same.

Examples: If one rolls a die, each of the six numbers is equally likely to show on top.

If one rolls two dice and adds the top numbers, there are eleven possible totals, 2, 3, 4, 5, 6, 7, 8, 9, 10, 11, 12, and they are NOT equally likely. A 2 will happen only if one rolls 1 and 1, but a total of 7 will come from many pairs, 1 and 6, 2 and 5, 3 and 4, 4 and 3, 5 and 2, 6 and 1.

See **Probability**

Equation

An equation is a statement using an equals sign.

Examples:

$y = 3x$ $x + 4 = 7$

$y = x^2 - 5$ $2x + 5 = 7x$

See **Expression**

Relation as an equation

An equation is one way of showing a *relation*.

Examples:

The *linear relation* $x \rightarrow x + 3$

can be written as the *linear equation*. $y = x + 3$

The *quadratic relation*

can be written as the equation. $x \rightarrow x^2 + 2$

(This is NOT called a quadratic equation.) $y = x^2 + 2$

See **Equation of a line, Linear equation, Quadratic equation, Simultaneous equations, Solution of an equation**

Equation of a line

The equation of a line is the *relation* satisfied by the *coordinates* of the points of the line.

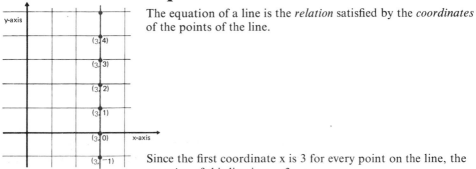

Since the first coordinate x is 3 for every point on the line, the *equation* of this line is x = 3.

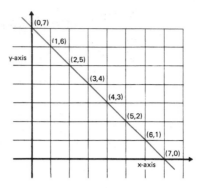

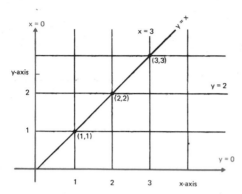

Since the two coordinates always add up to 7 for the points on this line, its equation is
$$x + y = 7.$$

NOTE: The equation of the x-*axis* is $y = 0$, and the equation of the y-axis is $x = 0$.

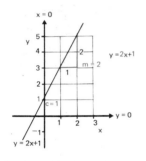

Any straight line on a *graph* represents a *linear equation*, which can be written in the form $y = mx + c$.

Examples:

$y = 3x - 4 \qquad y = x + 1$

$y = 8 - x \qquad y = 2 - \frac{1}{2}x$

When a linear equation is written in the form $y = mx + c$, the number m represents the *gradient* of the line, and the number c represents the *intercept* on the y-*axis*.

Equilateral triangle

An equilateral triangle is a *triangle* with all three sides the same length.

Examples:

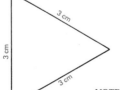

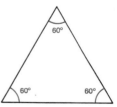

NOTE: If all three sides of a triangle are equal, the *angles* will be equal and will be 60°.

Equivalent fractions

Fractions are equivalent if they can be *canceled* to the same fraction, that is, if they name the same number.

Example: $\frac{8}{12}$ and $\frac{6}{9}$ are equivalent because they can both be canceled to $\frac{2}{3}$.

Here are two *sets* of equivalent fractions:

$$\left\{ \frac{1}{2}, \quad \frac{2}{4}, \quad \frac{4}{8}, \quad \frac{5}{10}, \quad \frac{8}{16}, \quad \frac{10}{20} \right\}$$

$$\left\{ \frac{5}{6}, \quad \frac{50}{60}, \quad \frac{10}{12}, \quad \frac{25}{30}, \quad \frac{500}{600} \right\}$$

If $\frac{a}{b}$ is any fraction, then $\frac{ka}{kb}$ is an equivalent fraction where k is a number not equal to *zero*.

Euler's formula

Euler's *formula* applies to *networks* and to *polyhedra*.

For networks:

It relates the number of *nodes*, *regions*, and *arcs*.

nodes + regions − arcs = 2

N   + R   − A   = 2

Example:

There are 4 nodes A, B, C, and D.
There are 7 arcs p, q, r, s, t, u, v.
There are 5 regions i, ii, iii, iv, vi.

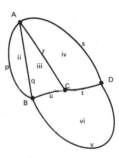

For polyhedra:

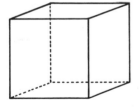

Euler's formula relates the number of vertices, faces, and edges.

vertices + faces − edges = 2

V   + F   − E   = 2

Example: A *cube* has 8 vertices, 6 faces, 12 edges.

Evaluate

Evaluate means *find the value of*.

Example: Evaluate 2a + b when a = 7, and b = 6.

$$
\begin{aligned}
2a + b &= 2 \times a + b \\
&= 2 \times 7 + 6 \\
&= 14 + 6 \\
&= 20
\end{aligned}
$$

Even numbers

Even numbers are numbers that can be divided exactly by 2. Even numbers are numbers ending in 0 or 2 or 4 or 6 or 8.

Examples: These are even numbers:

24, 750, 38, 6, 7914, 2908, 3100, 14.

The even numbers are the *multiples* of 2.

Exponent

A number x written as the *power* of another number a is called an exponent.

$49 = 7^2$
$16 = 2^4$
$10,000 = 10^4$
$125 = 5^3$
$0.01 = 10^{-2}$

If $x = a^n$, then n is the exponent showing the power of a.

Examples (left):

These numbers are written in exponential form; the exponents are shown in red.

See **Power of a number**

Expression

A collection of numbers and *symbols* and letters with NO equals sign is called an expression.

Examples:

$2x + 5 + 7x$
$a + b + 3b - a$
$2 \sin x$
$x^2 + 1$

Statements which DO have an equals sign are called *equations*.

Faces

The flat sides of a *polyhedron* are called faces.

Examples:

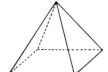

This *pyramid* has five faces (four sides and one base).

This solid figure has six faces.

This *prism* has five faces.

Factoring

Factoring is the process of writing a number or an expression as a product of *factors*.

When we use the distributive property backwards, we call it factoring.

Examples:

ab + ac = a(b + c)

3x + 3y = 3(x + y)

7 × 53 + 7 × 47 = 7 × (53 + 47) = 7 × 100

PR + QR = (P + Q)R

$(A \cap B) \cup (A \cap C) = A \cap (B \cup C)$

Factors

The factors of a number are those numbers that divide exactly into the number.

Example: The factors of 24 are 1, 2, 3, 4, 6, 8, 12, 24.

See **Prime factors**

Pair of factors

The pairs of factors of 30 are 1 × 30, 2 × 15, 3 × 10, 5 × 6

Set of factors

The *set* of factors of 30 are {1, 2, 3, 5, 6, 10, 15, 30}

Prime factors

Prime factors are factors that are prime numbers.
The prime factors of 30 are 2, 3, and 5 (NOT 1, 6, 10, 15, 30).

Fibonacci numbers

A Fibonacci number is one from this *set* of numbers,

$$\{ \ 1, \quad 1, \quad 2, \quad 3, \quad 5, \quad 8, \quad 13, \quad 21, \quad \ldots \ \}$$

$$1 + 1 = 2$$

$$1 + 2 = 3$$

$$2 + 3 = 5$$

$$3 + 5 = 8$$

Each number is the *sum* of the two numbers before it.

Formula

A formula is a general *equation*. It shows the connection between related quantities.

Example: The *perimeter* P of a *rectangle* with sides a and b is given by the formula
P = 2a + 2b

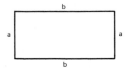

Some examples of formulas you may meet are:

$$v = u + at; C = \pi d; T = 2\pi \sqrt{\frac{l}{g}}; \frac{1}{f} = \frac{1}{v} + \frac{1}{u};$$

$A = \pi r^2$; and *Euler's formula* $N + R - A = 2$.

Fraction

A fraction is a number less than 1. It names part of a region or part of a group.

$$\frac{1}{2} \qquad \frac{1}{4} \qquad \frac{3}{5} \qquad \frac{11}{13} \qquad \frac{21}{40}$$

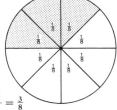

Example (above): $\dfrac{\text{number of shaded parts}}{\text{number of parts of circle}} = \frac{3}{8}$

The shaded portion of the *circle* is $\frac{3}{8}$ of the whole circle.

NOTE: The bottom number of a fraction is called the *denominator*, and the top number is called the *numerator*.

See **Decimal fraction, Equivalent fractions, Improper fraction, Percent fraction**

Frequency

The frequency of an event, or outcome, is how many times it has happened.

Example: A die is rolled 100 times, and a six comes up 13 times. The frequency of the outcome six is 13.

See **Histogram, Mode**

Frequency diagram

A frequency diagram is a *bar graph* showing *frequency*.
The height of the bars shows the frequency of each event.

Example: A die is rolled 130 times.

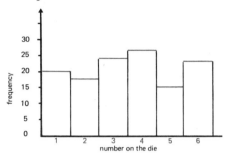

See **Histogram**

Function

$$x \xrightarrow{f} x$$
$$^{+}2 \searrow 4$$
$$^{-}2 \nearrow 4$$
$$3 \to 9$$
$$4 \to 16$$

Functions are special kinds of *relations* in which each *object* is *mapped onto* only ONE *image*.
Functions are also known as *mappings*.

Examples:
f (*left*) is a function, as every object has only ONE image.

However, g (*below*) is NOT a function, as there is more than one image for each object.

$$x \xrightarrow{g} \text{square root of } x$$
$$1 \to {}^{+}1 \text{ or } {}^{-}1$$
$$4 \to {}^{+}2 \text{ or } {}^{-}2$$
$$9 \to {}^{+}3 \text{ or } {}^{-}3$$

See **Correspondence** and **Mapping**

Glide reflection

The glide reflection is the *transformation* that will replace the combined transformations: a *translation parallel* to line m and a *reflection* in line m, taken in either order.

Examples:

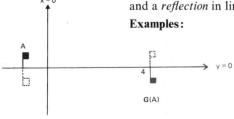

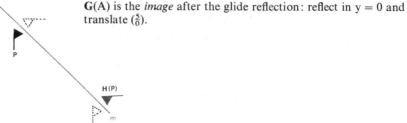

G(A) is the *image* after the glide reflection: reflect in y = 0 and translate $\binom{5}{0}$.

H(P) is the image after the glide reflection: translate parallel to m and reflect in line m.

Gradient

The gradient of a line is a measurement of how steep it is. The gradient of a line can be found by drawing *right triangles* on the line.

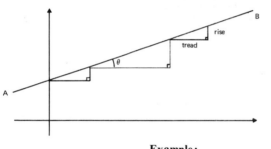

Gradient of line AB $= \dfrac{\text{rise}}{\text{tread}}$

$= \tan \theta$

Example:
Gradient of y = 2x is

$$\frac{\text{rise}}{\text{tread}} = \frac{6}{3} = \frac{2}{1} = 2.$$

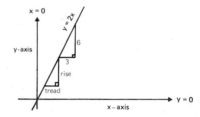

Gram

A gram is a *unit* of mass. A gram weight is the weight of a mass of one gram. A large pea has a mass of about 1 g.

Example:

A spoon has a mass of about 17 g.

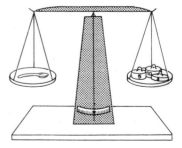

Graph

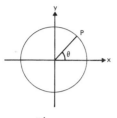

A graph is a way of illustrating information and numbers (data) on paper to make it more easily understood.

Data are often displayed by *bar graphs, circle graphs, frequency diagrams, histograms,* and *pictograms.*

In other situations *axes* and *coordinates* are used.

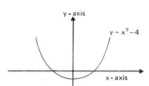

Greatest common factor

Two *counting numbers* always have 1 as a common *factor.* Often they will have other factors in common.

Example:
{factors of 12} = {1, 2, 3, 4, 6, 12}
{factors of 15} = {1, 3, 5, 15}
1 and 3 are the only common factors of 12 and 15.

The greatest common factor (usually abbreviated to GCF) is the largest of these numbers, in this case 3.

{factors of 20} = {1, 2, 4, 5, 10, 20}
{factors of 30} = {1, 2, 3, 5, 6, 10, 15, 30}
10 is the greatest common factor of 20 and 30.

Hemisphere

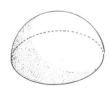

A hemisphere is half a *sphere,* formed by a *plane of symmetry* of the sphere.

Examples:

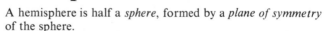

Heptagon

A heptagon is a *polygon* bounded by 7 straight lines and containing 7 *angles*.

Examples:

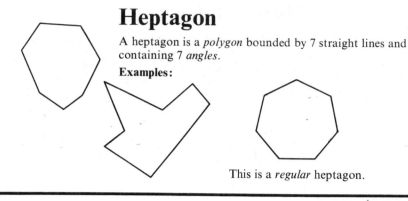

This is a *regular* heptagon.

Hexagon

A hexagon is a *polygon* bounded by 6 straight lines and containing 6 *angles*.

Examples:

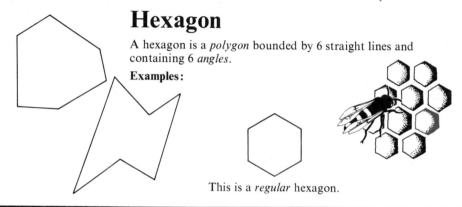

This is a *regular* hexagon.

Histogram

time interval 2 hours	frequency
9-11	610
11- 1	750
1- 3	500
3- 5	625
5- 7	145
7- 9	490

A histogram is similar to a *frequency diagram* and a *bar graph*. If the intervals (that which is being measured) are all equal, the height of the contiguous bars are an exact measure of the frequency (as in a bar graph).

If the intervals along the x axis are not all equal it is the *area* of the bars and not their height that shows the frequencies.

Example: The table (*left*) shows the frequency of shoppers at intervals of 2 hours, starting at 9 A.M.

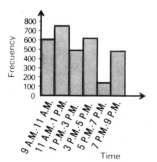

Horizontal

A line is horizontal if it is *parallel* to the ocean's skyline.

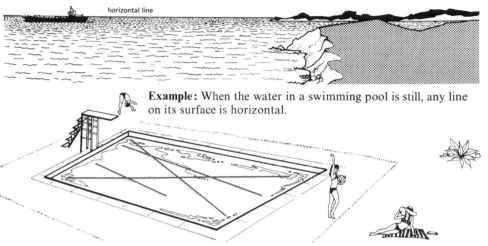

horizontal line

Example: When the water in a swimming pool is still, any line on its surface is horizontal.

Hypotenuse

The hypotenuse is the side opposite the *right angle* in a *right triangle*. It is also the longest side in a right triangle.

Examples:

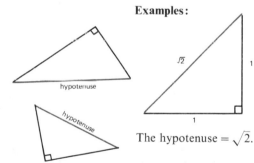

hypotenuse

hypotenuse

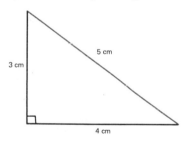

$\sqrt{2}$ 1

1

The hypotenuse = $\sqrt{2}$.

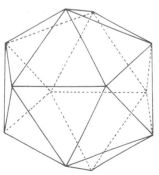

5 cm

3 cm

4 cm

The hypotenuse = 5 cm.

Icosahedron

An icosahedron is a solid with twenty *faces*.
In a *regular* icosahedron each face is an *equilateral triangle*.

Example (right):
This is a regular icosahedron.

45

Identical

Shapes and objects are identical if they are exactly the same shape and size.

In some *transformations*, such as *reflection* and *rotation*, the *object* and *image* are identical. These transformations are called *isometries*.

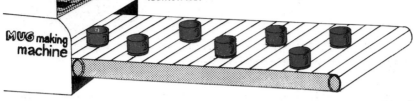

MUG making machine

Tessellations show patterns with one or more identical shapes, which fit together without gaps to fill space.

See **Congruent**

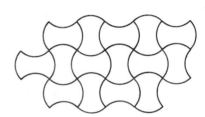

Identity element

An identity is an *element*, which when combined with other elements, leaves them the same. The identity depends on the *set* of elements and the *operation*.

Examples:

For numbers

and the operation ×
  it is 1
  $3 \times 1 = 3$
  $2 \times 1 = 2$
  $1 \times 5 = 5$
  $^{-}6 \times 1 = {}^{-}6$
  $1 \times 4 = 4$

and the operation +
  it is 0
  $0 + 3 = 3$
  $2 + 0 = 2$
  $0 + 5 = 5$
  $^{-}6 + 0 = {}^{-}6$
  $9 + 0 = 9$

For sets

and the operation ∪
  it is ϕ
  $A \cup \phi = A$
  $\phi \cup B = B$

and the operation ∩
  it is $\mathscr{E}$
  $P \cap \mathscr{E} = P$
  $\mathscr{E} \cap Q = Q$

For 2 by 2 matrices

and the operation addition, it is $\begin{pmatrix} 0 & 0 \\ 0 & 0 \end{pmatrix}$

and the operation multiplication, it is $\begin{pmatrix} 1 & 0 \\ 0 & 1 \end{pmatrix}$

Identity mapping

Identity mapping *maps* each *element* onto itself.

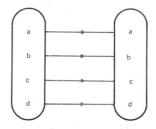

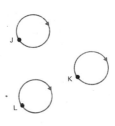

Identity transformation

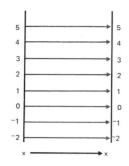

The identity transformation is the *transformation* that *maps* each point of the *plane* onto itself. Under the identity transformation a shape remains unchanged and all properties of the shape are *invariant*.

When *matrices* are used to represent transformations in the plane, the identity transformation is represented by the matrix $\begin{pmatrix} 1 & 0 \\ 0 & 1 \end{pmatrix}$

Image

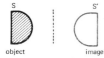

The image is the result when an *object* is *transformed*.

Examples: The shape S′ is the image in each case.

Here the image is the result of a *reflection*.

Here the image is the result of a *rotation* about 0.

The image is also the result when a number undergoes a *mapping*.

Examples:

$x \to x + 2$
$3 \to 5$
$2 \to 4$ the image of 3 is 5
$5 \to 7$ the image of 1 is 3
$1 \to 3$ the image of 6 is 8
$0 \to 2$
$6 \to 8$

NOTE: The *set* of images {5, 4, 7, 3, 2, 8} is called the image set.

See **Corresponding points**

Improper fraction

An improper fraction is a *fraction* whose *numerator* is larger than the *denominator*, such as

$$\frac{5}{3}, \quad \frac{7}{4}, \quad \frac{10}{9}, \quad \frac{16}{13}, \quad \frac{8}{5}, \quad \frac{11}{5}$$

These improper fractions can be rewritten as *mixed numbers*.

Examples:

$$\frac{5}{3} = 1\frac{2}{3}, \quad \frac{7}{4} = 1\frac{3}{4}, \quad \frac{10}{9} = 1\frac{1}{9},$$
$$\frac{16}{13} = 1\frac{3}{13}, \quad \frac{8}{5} = 1\frac{3}{5}, \quad \frac{11}{5} = 2\frac{1}{5}$$

Incidence matrix

An incidence *matrix* relates *nodes*, *arcs*, *regions*, and other properties of a *network*.

Example:

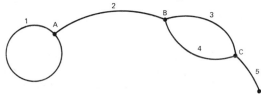

The nodes are lettered A, B, C, and D.
The arcs are numbered 1, 2, 3, 4, and 5.

For this network the incidence of nodes on arcs is shown by the matrix

$$
\mathbf{P} = \begin{array}{c} \\ A \\ B \\ C \\ D \end{array}
\begin{pmatrix}
1 & 2 & 3 & 4 & 5 \\
2 & 1 & 0 & 0 & 0 \\
0 & 1 & 1 & 1 & 0 \\
0 & 0 & 1 & 1 & 1 \\
0 & 0 & 0 & 0 & 1
\end{pmatrix}
$$

The *transpose* of **P**, **P′**, shows the incidence of arcs on nodes. The matrix *product* **PP′** is the same as the *route matrix* **R** for the nodes A, B, C, and D, except that the *leading diagonal* is different.

$$
\mathbf{PP'} =
\begin{pmatrix}
2 & 1 & 0 & 0 & 0 \\
0 & 1 & 1 & 1 & 0 \\
0 & 0 & 1 & 1 & 1 \\
0 & 0 & 0 & 0 & 1
\end{pmatrix}
\begin{pmatrix}
2 & 0 & 0 & 0 \\
1 & 1 & 0 & 0 \\
0 & 1 & 1 & 0 \\
0 & 1 & 1 & 0 \\
0 & 0 & 1 & 1
\end{pmatrix}
=
\begin{pmatrix}
3 & 1 & 0 & 0 \\
1 & 3 & 2 & 0 \\
0 & 2 & 3 & 1 \\
0 & 0 & 1 & 1
\end{pmatrix}
$$

$$
\text{but} \quad \mathbf{R} =
\begin{pmatrix}
2 & 1 & 0 & 0 \\
1 & 0 & 2 & 0 \\
0 & 2 & 0 & 1 \\
0 & 0 & 1 & 0
\end{pmatrix}
$$

Inequality

An inequality is a statement showing that one quantity is NOT equal to another quantity.

a < b means a is less than b
a > b means a is greater than b
a ≠ b means a is not equal to b

Examples:
From the dots on the number line (*left*) it can be seen that

4 > 1	1 < 4
1 > ⁻2	⁻2 < 1
⁻2 > ⁻5	⁻5 < ⁻2

The *solution* to the inequality x < 3 is shown by the red line (*right*).

See **Integers, Solution set**

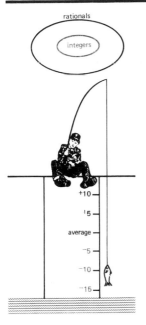

Integers

The *set* of integers is $\{\ldots{}^-4,\ ^-3,\ ^-2,\ ^-1,\ 0,\ 1,\ 2,\ 3,\ldots\}$

The set of integers is a *subset* of the set of *rational numbers.*

The set of *counting numbers* is a subset of the set of integers.

Examples:

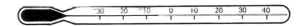

The *set* of numbers used for the higher readings are called *positive* integers and are sometimes marked with a ⁺, like this:
$\{^+1,\ ^+2,\ ^+3,\ ^+4,\ ^+5,\ ^+6,\ \ldots\}$
The set of numbers for the lower readings are called *negative* integers and are marked with a ⁻, like this:
$\{^-1,\ ^-2,\ ^-3,\ ^-4,\ ^-5,\ ^-6,\ \ldots\}$

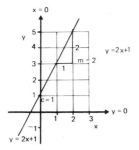

Intercept

An intercept is the point where the graph of an equation crosses an axis.

Example (left):
In this case 1 is the intercept on the y-axis.

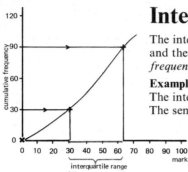

interquartile range
31   63

Interquartile range

The interquartile range is the *range* of the *data* between the first and the third *quartiles*. It is usually found from a *cumulative frequency* diagram.

Example (left):
The interquartile range is $63 - 31 = 32$ marks.
The semi-interquartile range is $\frac{1}{2} \times (63 - 31) = 16$ marks.

Intersect

Lines and curves intersect if they cross or touch.

Examples (left):
Lines p and q intersect at A;
the *circle* and line q intersect at B;
but the line p and the circle do not intersect.

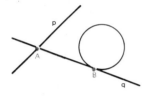

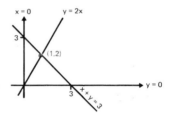

(*Right*) Lines $y = 2x$ and $x + y = 3$ intersect at the point (1, 2).

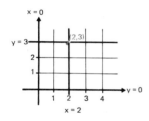

(*Left*) Point (2,3) is the *intersection* of line $x = 2$ and line $y = 3$.

Intersection

The intersection of two *sets* A and B is the set that has in it only those *elements* that are in both set A and set B.

Example:
If $A = \{2,4,6,8\}$
and $B = \{1,2,4,8\}$ The intersection of sets is shown by
then $A \cap B = \{2,4,8\}$ the **symbol** $\cap$.

On a *Venn diagram*, the intersection of set A and set B is shown by the set of points shaded red. $A \cap B$ *is shaded red.*

Invariants

Invariants are properties of the *object* and *image* that are the same both BEFORE and AFTER the transformation, such as length, *area*, *angles*, *parallel* lines, straightness, number of *arcs*, and *sense*.

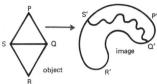

Examples:
For a *topological transformation*, some invariants are *order of nodes*, number of arcs, *regions*, and nodes.

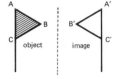

For a *reflection*, some invariants are straightness, size of angle, area, and number of regions. But sense is changed, so sense is not an invariant.

Inverse element

The inverse of an *element* is the element that combines with it to give the *identity*.
If a *set* has no *identity element* under an *operation*, there are NO inverses.

Examples:
For numbers under addition:
the inverse of 6 is $^-6$ because $6 + {}^-6 = 0$
the inverse of 3 is $^-3$ because $3 + {}^-3 = 0$
the inverse of $^-1$ is 1 because $^-1 + 1 = 0$

$\left\{\begin{array}{l}\text{and because 0 is}\\ \text{the identity for}\\ \text{numbers under}\\ \text{addition.}\end{array}\right.$

For 2 by 2 *matrices* and multiplication:

the inverse of $\begin{pmatrix} 3 & 1 \\ 5 & 2 \end{pmatrix}$ is $\begin{pmatrix} 2 & {}^-1 \\ {}^-5 & 3 \end{pmatrix}$

because $\begin{pmatrix} 3 & 1 \\ 5 & 2 \end{pmatrix}\begin{pmatrix} 2 & {}^-1 \\ -5 & 3 \end{pmatrix} = \begin{pmatrix} 1 & 0 \\ 0 & 1 \end{pmatrix}$

the inverse of $\begin{pmatrix} 1 & 0 \\ 7 & 6 \end{pmatrix}$ is $\frac{1}{6}\begin{pmatrix} 6 & 0 \\ -7 & 1 \end{pmatrix}$

because $\begin{pmatrix} 1 & 0 \\ 7 & 6 \end{pmatrix}\begin{pmatrix} 1 & 0 \\ -\frac{7}{6} & \frac{1}{6} \end{pmatrix} = \begin{pmatrix} 1 & 0 \\ 0 & 1 \end{pmatrix}$

and because $\begin{pmatrix} 1 & 0 \\ 0 & 1 \end{pmatrix}$ is the identity for 2 by 2 matrices and multiplication

If $\mathbf{M} = \begin{pmatrix} a & b \\ c & d \end{pmatrix}$ then,

the inverse of $\mathbf{M}$ is $\mathbf{M}^{-1} = \dfrac{1}{\det \mathbf{M}}\begin{pmatrix} d & {}^-b \\ {}^-c & a \end{pmatrix}$ where

$\det \mathbf{M}$ is the *determinant* of the matrix $\mathbf{M}$.

Inverse function

As the words *functions* and *mapping* have the same meaning, an inverse function is the same as an *inverse mapping*.

Example: For $x \xrightarrow{f} 2x$ the inverse function is $x \xrightarrow{f^{-1}} \frac{1}{2}x$

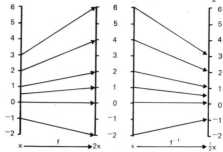

NOTE: A *function* f is either a MANY-TO-ONE or a ONE-TO-ONE *correspondence*; BUT f can only have an *inverse function* if f is a ONE-TO-ONE correspondence.

Inverse pair

If an *element* has an *inverse* under an *operation*, the element and its inverse are an inverse pair.

Examples: Some inverse pairs for numbers under addition are $(6, {}^-6)$, $({}^-2, 2)$, $(\frac{1}{3}, {}^-\frac{1}{3})$, $({}^-1, 1)$.

When an element is its own inverse, the element is called self inverse.

Example:

$$\begin{pmatrix} {}^-1 & 0 \\ 0 & {}^-1 \end{pmatrix}\begin{pmatrix} {}^-1 & 0 \\ 0 & {}^-1 \end{pmatrix} = \begin{pmatrix} 1 & 0 \\ 0 & 1 \end{pmatrix} \text{ so } \begin{pmatrix} {}^-1 & 0 \\ 0 & {}^-1 \end{pmatrix} \text{is self inverse.}$$

Inverse transformation

For a *transformation* **M** that *maps* point P onto its *image* P', the inverse transformation $\mathbf{M}^{-1}$ is the transformation that maps P' back onto P, for all points.

Example: The transformation **E**: *enlargement* with *scale factor* 2 about O, has the inverse transformation $\mathbf{E}^{-1}$: enlargement with scale factor $\frac{1}{2}$ about O.

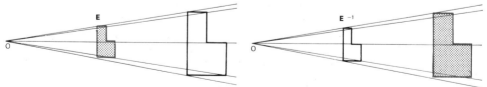

NOTE: If a transformation is represented by the *matrix* A, the inverse transformation, when it exists, is represented by the *inverse* matrix $\mathbf{A}^{-1}$.

Irrational numbers

An irrational number is a number that cannot be written as a *fraction*, $\frac{p}{q}$, where p and q are *integers* and q is not *zero*.

Examples:

$\sqrt{2} = 1.414\ldots$

$\pi = 3.14159265\ldots$

$\sqrt{10} = 3.1623\ldots$

$(\sqrt{7} + 8) = 10.6458\ldots$

When irrational numbers are expressed as decimals, they do NOT *terminate*.

The *symbol* I is sometimes used for the *set* of irrational numbers. The *union* of the *rational* numbers and the irrational numbers is the set of *real numbers*.

$I \cup Q = R$

See **Rational numbers**

Isometric

Isometric paper is paper covered with a *tessellation* of *equilateral triangles*.

Example: This is $\frac{1}{2}$ cm isometric paper. Each side of every triangle is $\frac{1}{2}$ cm.

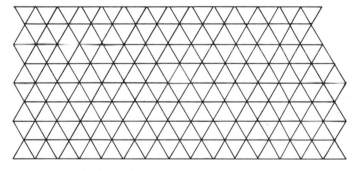

Isometries

Isometries are the *transformations* in which all lengths are *invariant*.

Examples: *Rotations*, *reflections*, and *translations* are isometries. An isometry in which *sense* is invariant is called a direct isometry. An isometry that doesn't preserve sense is called an opposite isometry.

After the *identity transformation*, the isometries are the simplest transformations for the *map* figures of the same shape and size.

See **Similarities**

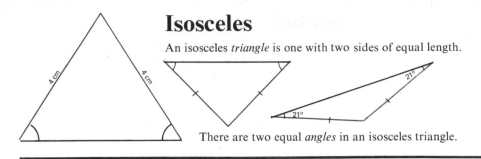

Isosceles

An isosceles *triangle* is one with two sides of equal length.

There are two equal *angles* in an isosceles triangle.

Journey

A journey is another word for a *displacement*.

Kilogram

A kilogram is a standard *unit* of mass. It is equal to 1,000 *grams*. We shorten kilogram to kg.

Examples:
A bag of potatoes may be 5 kg.
                    A man may be 70 kg.

1,000 g = 1 kg
1,000 kg = 1 *tonne* (metric ton)

Kilometer

A kilometer is a length of 1,000 *meters*. We shorten kilometer to km. One kilometer is a distance of a little over $\frac{1}{2}$ a mile.

Example: The red line shows 1 kilometer.

Latitude

A parallel of latitude is a *circle* on the surface of the earth, with a center on the line joining North and South Poles. These circles are all *parallel* to each other and so are called parallels of latitude.

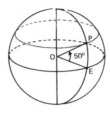 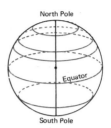

To describe any point P on the parallel of latitude shown in red, we use the *angle* between the two *radii* of the earth OP and OE. O is the center of the earth, and E is the point on the Equator, thus P and E are on the same line of *longitude*. The red circle is called the parallel of latitude 50°N. Other parallels are similarly labeled.

Leading diagonal

In a table or *matrix* that is *square*, the line of numbers or letters going from the top left corner to the bottom right corner is called the leading diagonal.

Examples:

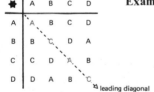 

Least common multiple

For two (or more) numbers a and b, the common *multiples* are those numbers which appear in both the *set* of multiples of a and the set of multiples of b.

Example:
{multiples of 2} = {2, 4, 6, 8, 10, 12, 14, 16, 18, 20, 22, 24,...}
{multiples of 3} = {3, 6, 9, 12, 15, 18, 21, 24, 27,...}
{common multiples of 2 and 3} = {6, 12, 18, 24,...}

The least common multiple (usually abbreviated to LCM) is the smallest of the common multiples.

Examples:
The LCM of 2 and 3 is 6
The LCM of 4 and 8 is 8
The LCM of 10 and 15 is 30
The LCM of 5 and 7 is 35

Line segment

A line segment is a part of a straight line between two given points.

Example:

A — B

AB is a line segment

Line of symmetry

A line of *symmetry* on a shape is a line that can be used as a fold, so that one half of the shape covers the other half exactly. A shape may have one or more lines of symmetry.

Examples:

| one line of symmetry | two lines of symmetry | three lines of symmetry | no line of symmetry |

A line of symmetry is also called reflective symmetry because a mirror *reflection* on the line will produce the whole shape.

Linear equation

A linear equation with ONE unknown (letter) is an *equation* that can be written in the form
$ax + b = 0$

Examples:
$3x + 4 = 7$ $2x + 6 = x - 2$
These equations can have only ONE *solution*.

When a linear equation is used to show a *linear relation*, the equation can be written with the two unknowns x and y in the form
$y = ax + b$
In this there are many solutions. See **Equation of a line**

Linear relations

Linear relations are *relations* that can be written in the form
x → ax + b. When *ordered pairs* for a linear relation are plotted
on a *graph*, they form a straight line.

Examples: Here are some linear relations:

x → x + 2

x → 3x

x → 4x − 1

x → 5 − $\frac{1}{2}$x

Linear scale factor see Scale factor

Liter

A liter is a *unit* of *volume* equal to 1,000 *cubic centimeters*.

Examples:

1 quart is a little
less than 1 liter.

Locus (plural Loci)

The locus is the line, or path, of a *set* of points that follow some
rule or law.

Example:
If Q is a fixed point, and {P: PQ is 2 cm}, then the locus of P
is a *circle*.

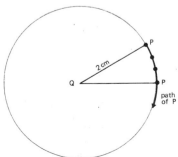

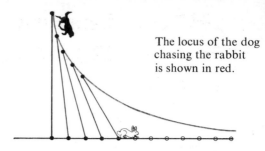

The locus of the dog chasing the rabbit is shown in red.

The locus of the man as the ladder slips down is shown in red.

Logarithm function

The logarithm function is the *inverse* of a growth *function*.
The term logarithm is shortened to log.

If $x \xrightarrow{f} a^x$, then $x \xrightarrow{f^{-1}} \log_a x$.

Example: For the growth function $x \rightarrow 2^x$ the inverse function is $x \rightarrow \log_2 x$

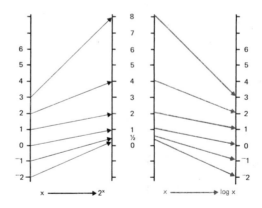

In the above example the logarithm function is to *base* 2; because we count in a base ten number system, for computation work, we use only the logarithm function to base 10.
$x \rightarrow \log_{10} x$,
which is the inverse function of $x \rightarrow 10^x$.

Examples:

$x \rightarrow 10^x$	$x \rightarrow \log x$
$2 \rightarrow 10^2$	$100 \rightarrow 2$
$3 \rightarrow 10^3$	$1{,}000 \rightarrow 3$
$^-1 \rightarrow 0.1$	$0.1 \rightarrow {}^-1$
$0.301 \rightarrow 10^{0.301}$	$2 \rightarrow 0.301$
$0.301 \rightarrow 2$	

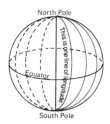

North Pole

This is one line of longitude

Equator

South Pole

Longitude

A line of longitude is half a *circle* on the surface of the earth, with one end at the South Pole and one end at the North Pole.

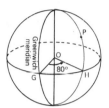

To describe any point P on the line of longitude shown in red, we use the *angle* between the *radii* OG and OH. O is the center of the earth, G and H are points on the Equator, and H is also on the red line of longitude. G is on the black line of longitude, called the Greenwich meridian, or 0° longitude. It is the line of longitude that passes through Greenwich, a suburb of London, England.

Mapping

A mapping is a *relation* in which for each *object mapped* there is only ONE *image*.

Examples (left and right):

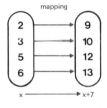

mapping

2	9
3	10
5	12
6	13

x ⟶ x+7

See **Correspondence** and **Function**

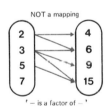

NOT a mapping

2	4
3	6
5	9
7	15

'— is a factor of —'

Mapping diagram

A mapping diagram is a diagram to show a *mapping*. We can use a *relation diagram* to do this, but usually we use two number lines and arrows.

Example:

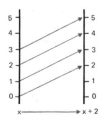

x ⟶ x + 2

Maps (onto)

A *transformation* maps an *object* onto its *image*.

Example: point A, (1, 2) is MAPPED ONTO point A′, (3, 6) by the *translation* $\binom{2}{4}$.

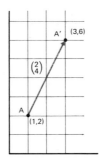

Matrix (plural **Matrices**)

A matrix is an array of numbers or letters in the shape of a *rectangle*.

Examples:

$$\begin{pmatrix} 1 & 0 & 0 & 1 \\ 0 & 2 & 1 & 1 \\ 0 & 1 & 0 & 3 \\ 1 & 1 & 3 & 0 \end{pmatrix} \quad \begin{pmatrix} 1 & 2 \\ 7 & \frac{2}{3} \end{pmatrix} \quad \begin{pmatrix} a & d \\ b & a \\ a & c \end{pmatrix}$$

Each number or letter is called an *element* of the matrix.

Addition of matrices

Matrices can be added, if they have the same *order*, by adding corresponding elements.

Example:

$$\begin{pmatrix} 2 & 3 & 1 \\ 0 & 4 & 0 \end{pmatrix} + \begin{pmatrix} 7 & 1 & 1 \\ 1 & 0 & 0 \end{pmatrix} = \begin{pmatrix} 9 & 4 & 2 \\ 1 & 4 & 0 \end{pmatrix}$$

Multiplication of matrices

Two matrices **A** and **B** can be multiplied if the number of elements in the *columns* of **A** equals the number of elements in the *rows* of **B**.

To form the *product* **AB** the orders of the matrices **A** and **B** must fit the pattern

$$\underset{\text{p by q}}{\mathbf{A}} \quad \underset{\text{q by r}}{\mathbf{B}} \quad = \quad \underset{\text{p by r}}{\mathbf{AB}}$$

When we multiply two matrices **A** and **B**, we combine each row of **A** with each column of **B**.

Example:

If $A = \begin{pmatrix} 3 & 0 & 4 \\ 2 & 1 & 1 \end{pmatrix}$

2 by 3

and $B = \begin{pmatrix} 1 & 1 \\ 3 & 1 \\ 2 & 5 \end{pmatrix}$

3 by 2

then $AB = \begin{pmatrix} 3 & 0 & 4 \\ 2 & 1 & 1 \end{pmatrix} \begin{pmatrix} 1 & 1 \\ 3 & 1 \\ 2 & 5 \end{pmatrix}$

$$= \begin{pmatrix} 3 \times 1 + 0 \times 3 + 4 \times 2 & 3 \times 1 + 0 \times 1 + 4 \times 5 \\ 2 \times 1 + 1 \times 3 + 1 \times 2 & 2 \times 1 + 1 \times 1 + 1 \times 5 \end{pmatrix}$$

2 by 2

the first row of **A** combines with the first column of **B**

to give $(3 \quad 0 \quad 4) \begin{pmatrix} 1 \\ 3 \\ 2 \end{pmatrix} = 3 + 0 + 8 = 11.$

Combining the other rows and columns in a similar way
gives $AB = \begin{pmatrix} 11 & 23 \\ 7 & 8 \end{pmatrix}$

In this example it would also be possible to compute
BA to obtain $\begin{pmatrix} 5 & 1 & 5 \\ 11 & 1 & 13 \\ 16 & 5 & 13 \end{pmatrix}$

NOTE: In general, matrix multiplication is NOT *commutative*. If it is possible to form the product **BA** as well as **AB,** usually **BA ≠ AB.**

For the *identity* and *inverse* of 2 by 2 matrices under multiplication, see **Identity element** and **Inverse element.**

Matrix transformation

Matrices can be used to represent *transformations* of the *plane*. When (x, y) is an *object* point and (x′, y′) is the *image* point, then a matrix *equation* of the form

$$\begin{pmatrix} x' \\ y' \end{pmatrix} = \begin{pmatrix} a & b \\ c & d \end{pmatrix} \begin{pmatrix} x \\ y \end{pmatrix}$$

can be used to represent transformations such as *reflections*, *shears*, and *enlargements*.

Examples:

$$\begin{pmatrix} x' \\ y' \end{pmatrix} = \begin{pmatrix} 0 & ^-1 \\ 1 & 0 \end{pmatrix} \begin{pmatrix} x \\ y \end{pmatrix}$$

represents a $^+90°$ *rotation* about the *origin*.

$$\begin{pmatrix} x' \\ y' \end{pmatrix} = \begin{pmatrix} 5 & 8 \\ ^-2 & ^-3 \end{pmatrix} \begin{pmatrix} x \\ y \end{pmatrix}$$

represents a shear with *invariant* line $y = ^-\frac{1}{2}x$.

Mean

(More correctly its name is Arithmetic Mean).
The mean is usually called the average by most non-mathematicians.
The mean of a *set* of n numbers is the *sum* of the n numbers divided by n.

Example: The mean of 1, 4, 3, 0, 1, 2, 1, 4   (eight numbers)
is $(1 + 4 + 3 + 0 + 1 + 2 + 1 + 4) \div 8$
$= 16 \div 8$
$= 2$
2 is the mean.

Median

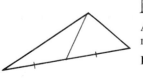

median
height

The median of a *set* of numbers is the MIDDLE NUMBER once the numbers have been arranged in order of size.

Examples:
a) The median of   2, 0, 3, 1, 4, 1, 5, 3, 2
   is found from   0, 1, 1, 2, 2, 3, 3, 4, 5

2 is the median

b) The median of   1, 4, 3, 0, 1, 2, 1, 4
   is found from   0, 1, 1, 1, 2, 3, 4, 4

There are two middle values, so $1\frac{1}{2}$ is the median.

NOTE: For a large collection of *data*, the median is the value for which half the data is greater and half the data is less. In this case, the data is usually found from a *cumulative frequency* curve.

See Quartile

Median of a triangle

A median of a triangle is the line drawn from a *vertex* to the midpoint of the side opposite.

Examples:

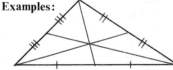

There are three *medians* for every triangle, one from each vertex, and all of them pass through the same point.

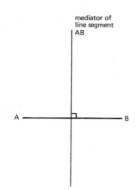

mediator of
line segment
AB

Mediator

The mediator of a *line* segment AB is the line which cuts AB in half at *right angles*.

The mediator is also the *line of symmetry* for the line segment.

Examples:

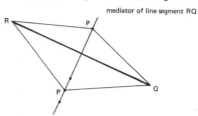

mediator of line segment RQ

NOTE: The *locus* of points P which are equidistant from R and Q is the mediator of RQ.

See **Bisector**

Member

The *elements* of a *set* are said to be members of the set.
The symbol for "is a member of" is ∈.

Examples:

Pig is a member of the set of animals

Pig ∈ {animals}

5 is a member of the set of counting numbers.

$5 \in \{1, 2, 3, 4, 5, 6, 7, 8, \ldots\}$

Meter

2 m

The meter is the standard *unit* of length. We shorten meter to m.

Example:

A door is about 2 meters high.

Millimeter

A millimeter is one thousandth of a *meter*. We shorten millimeter to mm.

$1 \text{ mm} = \dfrac{1}{1000} \text{ m}$

This gap is 1 millimeter.

Mixed number

A mixed number is a number that is a *whole number* with a *fraction*.

Examples:
$3\frac{1}{2}$, $2\frac{1}{5}$, $7\frac{3}{10}$, $4\frac{3}{5}$, $18\frac{3}{4}$

NOTE: $3\frac{1}{2}$ is the *sum* $3 + \frac{1}{2}$

See **Improper fraction**

Mode

The mode is the "most popular" value, or the most frequently occurring item.

Example:
For
    6, 7, 7, 8, 6, 5, 9, 8, 7, 6,
    5, 9, 8, 7, 4, 7, 8, 6, 8, 7,
    8, 5, 7, 7, 3, 7, 7, 3,

There are two 3s.
There is one 4.
There are three 5s.
There are four 6s.
There are ten 7s.   7 comes TEN times.
There are six 8s.
There are two 9s.

7 is the mode; it comes most often.

NOTE: If there are TEN 7s and TEN 8s, then both 7 and 8 are modes.

Motif

A motif is a small figure, or shape, that is repeated.

Example:
In this *tessellation*, the motif is

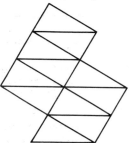

In a *pictogram* the motif is something suitable, such as an automobile or a person.

Multiple

A multiple of a number n is k × n where k is a *counting number*.

Examples:
Some multiples of 4 are 8, 12, 20, 24, 28
Some multiples of 5 are 5, 15, 20, 25, 35
{multiples of 3} = {3, 6, 9, 12, 15, 18, 21, 24,...}
{multiples of 7} = {7, 14, 21, 28, 35, 42,...}

Multiplicative inverse

A multiplicative inverse is an *inverse* under multiplication.

Examples:

For numbers

The multiplicative inverse of 3 is $\frac{1}{3}$ because $3 \times \frac{1}{3} = 1$
The multiplicative inverse of $\frac{1}{2}$ is 2 because $\frac{1}{2} \times 2 = 1$
The multiplicative inverse of $^-4$ is $^-\frac{1}{4}$ because $^-4 \times ^-\frac{1}{4} = 1$
and 1 is the *identity* for numbers under multiplication.

For 2 by 2 matrices

The multiplicative inverse of $\begin{pmatrix} 2 & 7 \\ 1 & 4 \end{pmatrix}$ is $\begin{pmatrix} 4 & ^-7 \\ ^-1 & 2 \end{pmatrix}$

because $\begin{pmatrix} 2 & 7 \\ 1 & 4 \end{pmatrix}\begin{pmatrix} 4 & ^-7 \\ ^-1 & 2 \end{pmatrix} = \begin{pmatrix} 1 & 0 \\ 0 & 1 \end{pmatrix}$ and $\begin{pmatrix} 1 & 0 \\ 0 & 1 \end{pmatrix}$

is the identity for 2 by 2 matrices under multiplication.

See **Inverse element**

Natural numbers

The *set* of natural numbers is another name for the set of *counting numbers*.
The set of natural numbers is {1, 2, 3, 4, 5, 6, 7,...}
The set of counting numbers is usually represented by the *symbol* N, and is a *subset* of the set of *integers*. See **Whole numbers.**

Negative numbers

Negative numbers are used to count or measure in the opposite sense to the *positive numbers*. They are marked with a $^-$ sign.
{negative *integers*} = {$^-1, ^-2, ^-3, ^-4, ^-5, ^-6, ^-7, ^-8, ...$}

Example: Point A is 3 above *zero* and is a positive number, 3.
Point B is 3 below zero and is a negative number, $^-3$.

NOTE: Negative numbers enable us to find an *additive inverse* for all *real numbers*.

See **Integers**

Net

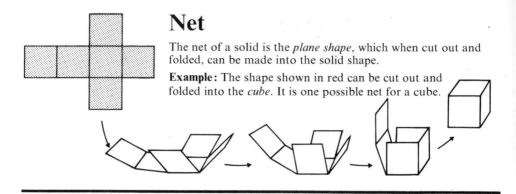

The net of a solid is the *plane shape*, which when cut out and folded, can be made into the solid shape.

Example: The shape shown in red can be cut out and folded into the *cube*. It is one possible net for a cube.

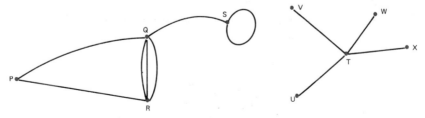

Network

A network is any diagram of connected lines.

Examples:

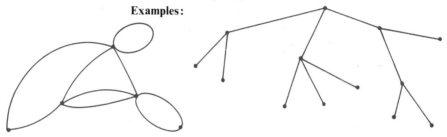

In any network the three main features are:
    the lines of the diagram, called *arcs*;
    the points at which the lines meet, called *nodes*;
    the areas for which the lines form a *boundary*, called *regions*.

See **Euler's formula, Incidence matrix, Node, Route matrix**

Node

A node is the point at the beginning and end of every *arc*. There must be a node where arcs meet on a *network*.

Examples:

P, Q, R, S, T, U, V, W, and X are nodes.

See **Order of a node**

Nonagon

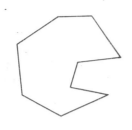

A nonagon is a *polygon* bounded by 9 straight lines and containing 9 *angles*.

Examples:

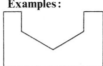

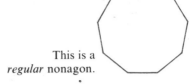

This is a
regular nonagon.

Numerator see **Fraction**

Object

In a *transformation* the shape or point being transformed is called the object.

Example:

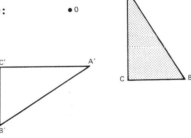

If the *triangle* ABC is *rotated* ⁻90° about 0, the result is triangle A′B′C′.

The shape ABC, shown in red, is called the object. The point A is an object point, for which A′ is its *image*.

See **Image**

In a *mapping* any number in the *set* being mapped is an object, but the whole set being mapped is usually called the *domain*.

Obtuse angle

An obtuse angle is an *angle* more than 90° but less than 180°.

Examples:

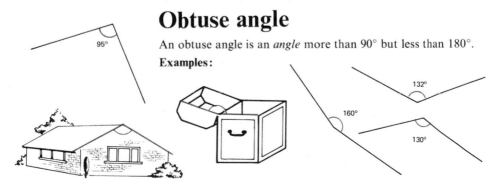

Octagon

An octagon is a *polygon* bounded by 8 straight lines and containing 8 *angles*.

Examples:

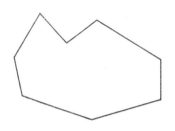 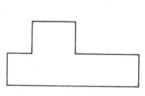 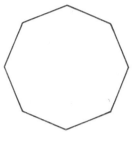

This is a *regular* octagon.

Octahedron

An octahedron is a solid shape with eight *faces*. In a *regular* octahedron each face is an *equilateral triangle*.

Examples:

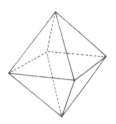 These are regular octahedrons.

Odd numbers

Odd numbers are *counting numbers* that are not *even*. Odd numbers do not divide exactly by 2. Odd numbers are those ending in 1 or 3 or 5 or 7 or 9.

Examples: These are odd numbers:

7, 13, 21, 39, 403, 60,827, 74,155, 200,461

Operation

An operation is a way of combining *elements* in a *set*. The most common kind of operation is a binary operation (binary meaning two). A binary operation combines two elements into one element.

Examples:

$\times$ is a binary operation on numbers

$4 \times 2 = 8$ $\frac{1}{2} \times 6 = 3$ $1 \times 9 = 9$ $3 \times \frac{1}{3} = 1$

+ is a binary operation on numbers

$$2 + 3 = 5 \qquad 1 + 7 = 8 \qquad 0 + 9 = 9 \qquad {}^-3 + 3 = 0$$

$\cup$ is a binary operation on sets

$$A \cup B = C \qquad A \cup C = D \qquad A \cup \phi = A$$

Many *sets* of *elements* have *operations* on them that show similar properties.

For an operation $*$ on a set, some of the properties we ask for are:

a) is the operation $*$ on the set *closed*?

b) is there an *identity* element in the set?

c) if there is an identity element, does each element of the set have an *inverse* in the set?

d) does the operation $*$ on the set show that it is
   i) *associative*?
   ii) *commutative*?
   and, when there is a second operation $\circ$ on the same set, that
   iii) $*$ is *distributive* over $\circ$?

A set with an operation that has the four properties of closure, identity, inverse, and associativity is called a group.

Examples:

The following sets with operations are each a group:

   Numbers under addition;
   Numbers (omitting *zero*) under multiplication;
   Vectors under addition;
   Isometries of the *plane* under "follows";
   The set of all 2 by 2 *matrices* (with *determinant* not zero) under matrix multiplication.

In a group, every *equation* $a * x = b$ or $x * a = b$ has a unique solution.

$+$ is a binary operation on *vectors*

$$\begin{pmatrix} 2 \\ 3 \end{pmatrix} + \begin{pmatrix} 5 \\ 1 \end{pmatrix} = \begin{pmatrix} 7 \\ 4 \end{pmatrix} \qquad\qquad \begin{pmatrix} 0 \\ 1 \end{pmatrix} + \begin{pmatrix} 5 \\ -6 \end{pmatrix} = \begin{pmatrix} 5 \\ -5 \end{pmatrix}$$

$$\begin{pmatrix} 0 \\ 0 \end{pmatrix} + \begin{pmatrix} 7 \\ 9 \end{pmatrix} = \begin{pmatrix} 7 \\ 9 \end{pmatrix}$$

multiplication is a binary operation on *matrices*

$$\begin{pmatrix} 1 & 1 \\ 2 & 3 \end{pmatrix}\begin{pmatrix} 4 & 1 \\ 0 & 2 \end{pmatrix} = \begin{pmatrix} 4 & 3 \\ 8 & 8 \end{pmatrix} \qquad \begin{pmatrix} 1 & 0 \\ 0 & 1 \end{pmatrix}\begin{pmatrix} 2 & 1 \\ 3 & 4 \end{pmatrix} = \begin{pmatrix} 2 & 1 \\ 3 & 4 \end{pmatrix}$$

Order of a matrix

The order of a matrix is the size of the *matrix*. If a matrix has m *rows* and n *columns*, then the matrix is of order m by n.

Examples:

A matrix of order 2 by 3 is this size $\begin{pmatrix} \square & \square & \square \\ \square & \square & \square \end{pmatrix}$

If $\mathbf{A} = \begin{pmatrix} 1 & 0 & 5 & 1 \\ 3 & 1 & 6 & 1 \\ 9 & 0 & 0 & 1 \end{pmatrix}$ then **A** is a 3 by 4 matrix.

If $\mathbf{B} = (7 \quad 8 \quad 1 \quad 5 \quad 0)$ then **B** is a 1 by 5 matrix.

Order of a node

The order of a *node* is the number of *arcs* that meet at the node. The order of a node can be found by counting the number of paths leaving the node.

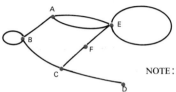

Examples:

A is a 3-node   D is a 1-node
B is a 4-node   E is a 5-node
C is a 3-node   F is a 2-node

NOTE: We usually ignore all 2-nodes such as F.

Ordered pairs

When we use pairs of numbers for which the order is important, they are called ordered pairs.

Examples:
Coordinates are ordered pairs: (3, 2) is not the same point as (2, 3). The order 3, 2 matters.

The ordered pair (1, 4) is a *solution* to the *equation* $y = x + 3$ because $\boxed{4} = \boxed{1} + 3$ but (4, 1) is not a solution $\boxed{1} \neq \boxed{4} + 3$; the order 1, 4 matters.

See Coordinates

Origin

The origin is the point with *coordinates* (0, 0).
It is the point where the *axes* cross. It is the point where the line x = 0 and the line y = 0 *intersect*.

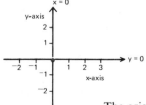

The origin is the point shown by the red dot.

Parabola

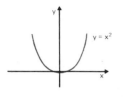

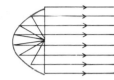

This is the shape obtained by plotting the *function* $x \rightarrow x^2$ using *coordinates*. It is also the shape for any function of the form $x \rightarrow ax^2 + bx + c$.

A parabola is a familiar shape, for it is approximately the path followed by a ball in flight; the shape of the wires supporting a suspension bridge; the cross section of the reflector for an electric heater.

Examples:

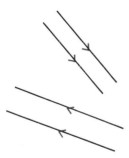

Parallel

Lines are parallel if they NEVER meet, no matter how far they are extended.

Examples: A pair of railway lines are parallel.

Parallel lines are always the same distance apart and they never *intersect*. Arrows are used to show parallel lines, as shown on the left.

Parallelogram

A parallelogram is a *quadrilateral* formed by two pairs of *parallel* lines. In general a parallelogram has:

a) NO *lines of symmetry*;
b) *rotational symmetry* of order 2;
c) opposite sides equal;
d) opposite angles of the figure equal;
e) *diagonals bisecting* each other.

Examples (left and right):

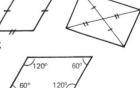

Parentheses ( ) (singular **Parenthesis**)

Parentheses are used when three or more *elements* are combined by *operations*. Parentheses tell you which two elements you combine first.

Example: $(10 - 7) + 2 = 3 + 2$
$$= 5$$
but
$$10 - (7 + 2) = 10 - 9$$
$$= 1$$

Pascal's triangle

Pascal's triangle is a pattern of numbers. The triangle pattern starts with the configuration below.

The general rule for continuing the pattern is: add each pair of numbers and write the result underneath, putting 1 at the beginning and 1 at the end.

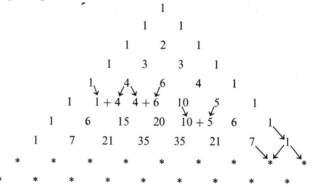

Pattern lines

Pattern lines are the lines used to draw an *enlargement*. They go through the center of enlargement and *corresponding points* in the shapes.

Example:

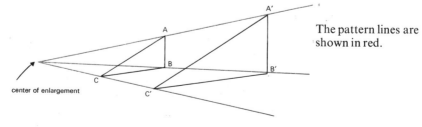

The pattern lines are shown in red.

Pentagon

A pentagon is a *polygon* bounded by 5 straight lines and containing 5 *angles*.

Examples:

This is a *regular* pentagon.

Percent

Percent is a ratio whose second term is 100. For example, 20 : 100, or 20 %. Percent means parts per hundred.

Examples: $\dfrac{20}{100} = 20 : 100 = 20\ \%$ $\dfrac{83}{100} = 83 : 100 = 83\ \%$

NOTE: (*Left*) % is 100 written in a special way.

Percent fraction

A percent fraction is a *fraction* with a *denominator* of 100.

Examples:

$$\frac{3}{100}, \frac{25}{100}, \frac{97}{100}, \frac{117}{100}, \frac{42\frac{1}{2}}{100}, \frac{350}{100}$$

By means of *equivalent fractions*, any fraction can be written as a percent fraction and as a *percent*.

Examples:

$$\frac{1}{4} = \frac{1 \times 25}{4 \times 25} = \frac{25}{100} = 25\ \% \qquad \frac{3}{8} = \frac{3 \times 12\frac{1}{2}}{8 \times 12\frac{1}{2}} = \frac{37\frac{1}{2}}{100} = 37\frac{1}{2}\ \%$$

$$\frac{2}{3} = \frac{2 \times 33\frac{1}{3}}{3 \times 33\frac{1}{3}} = \frac{66\frac{2}{3}}{100} = 66\frac{2}{3}\ \%$$

Perfect number

A perfect number is a *counting number* that equals the *sum* of all its *factors* except itself.

Examples:

6 {factors of 6} = {1, 2, 3, 6}
$\qquad\qquad\qquad\quad 1 + 2 + 3 = 6$

28 {factors of 28} = {1, 2, 4, 7, 14, 28}
$\qquad\qquad\qquad\quad 1 + 2 + 4 + 7 + 14 = 28$

NOTE: After 6 and 28 the next perfect number is 496.

73

Perimeter

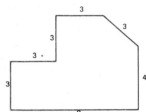

The perimeter of a figure, or shape, is the length of the distance around the outside of the shape.

Example (left):
Perimeter is $3 + 3 + 3 + 3 + 3 + 4 + 8 = 27$

Perpendicular

Lines are perpendicular if they cross at *right angles*.

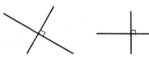

Similarly, *planes* are perpendicular if they meet at right angles. For example, in most rooms a wall and a floor are perpendicular.

Pi π

Pi is the *ratio* of the *circumference* of a *circle* to its *diameter*. For ALL circles the *fraction*

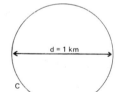

$$\frac{\text{circumference}}{\text{diameter}} \text{ is } \pi \qquad \frac{C}{d} = \pi \qquad \text{or} \qquad C = \pi d$$

$\pi = 3.141\ 592\ 653\ 589\ 79\ldots$

π is approximately
$\begin{aligned} &= 3 &&(1 \text{ significant figure}) \\ &= 3.1 &&(2 \text{ significant figures}) \\ &= 3.14 &&(3 \text{ significant figures}) \end{aligned}$

Another useful approximation for π is $3\frac{1}{7}$ or $\frac{22}{7}$.

Examples:

The distance around (C) a circular pond that is 1 km across is
$\begin{aligned} C &= \pi \times d \\ &= 3 \times 1 \\ &= 3 \text{ km (1 s.f.)} \end{aligned}$

The area of the same circular pond is
$\begin{aligned} A &= \pi \times r^2 \\ &= \pi \times 0.5^2 \\ &= 3.14 \times 0.25 \\ &= 0.7850 \text{ km}^2 \text{ (3 s.f.)} \end{aligned}$

Pictogram

A pictogram is a way of representing certain kinds of information. It is a form of graph. It is similar to a *bar graph* but uses a *motif*, or drawing.

Example (right):
Pictogram showing how pupils in grade 1 go to school.

walk	🚶🚶🚶🚶🚶🚶🚶🚶🚶🚶🚶
bus	🚶🚶🚶🚶
cycle	🚶🚶🚶🚶🚶

 represents 1 pupil

Plane

A *plane* is a flat surface like a tabletop.
A plane has no thickness and extends forever into space in all directions.

Example (left): When slicing a loaf of bread, the knife must be kept in one plane in order to get flat slices.

Plane shape

A plane shape is a shape that can be drawn with all its points in one *plane*.

Examples: All *polygons*, such as *squares* and *triangles*, are plane shapes, as are *circles*.

Plane of symmetry

A solid has a plane of symmetry if there is a *plane* which can act as a mirror to show the complete shape.

Examples (left and right):
For each solid the plane of symmetry is shown in red.

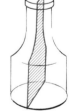

Point symmetry

A solid or plane shape has point *symmetry* if it can be given an *enlargement* with *scale factor* $^-1$ about one point so that the *image* occupies the same position as the *object*.

75

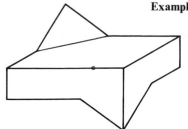

Examples:

This solid has
point symmetry
about the red dot.

This *plane shape* has
point symmetry
about the red dot.

If a plane shape has point symmetry, it has *rotational symmetry*
of *order 2*.

Polar coordinates

See **Coordinates** for Cartesian coordinates.

Polar coordinates are another way of describing the position of
points in a *plane*. Instead of (x, y), the distance r from the *origin*
and the *angle* θ from a fixed direction are given. The position
of a point P is then given by (r, θ) in polar coordinates.
(*Counter-clockwise* angles are indicated by *positive numbers*.)

Examples:

A is (2,30°).   B is (1,90°).
C is (3,150°).   D is (2,270°).

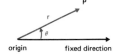

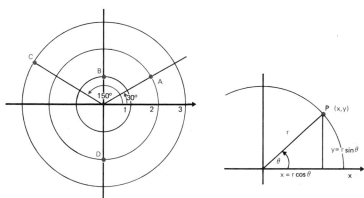

If P is (x, y) in Cartesian coordinates, and if P is (r, θ) in polar
coordinates, then

$$x = r \cos \theta, \quad y = r \sin \theta$$

and

$$r = \sqrt{x^2 + y^2}, \quad \tan \theta = \frac{y}{x}$$

Polygon

A polygon is a *plane shape* bounded by only straight lines.

Examples:

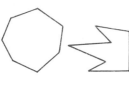

3 sides   triangle

4 sides   quadrilateral

5 sides   pentagon

6 sides   hexagon

7 sides   heptagon

8 sides   octagon

Polyhedron

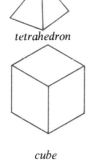

tetrahedron

A polyhedron is a solid shape with flat sides. The flat sides, or *faces*, are all *polygons*.

Examples: See **Cube, Dodecahedron, Icosahedron, Octahedron, Prism, Pyramid, Rectangular prism, Tetrahedron**

NOTE: There are only these five *regular* polyhedra:

cube

octahedron   *dodecahedron*   *icosahedron*

Positive numbers

Positive numbers are numbers greater than *zero*, such as
3,   2.56,   0.00081
On the number line any number to the right of zero (as shown by the red line) is a positive number.

$$^{-}3 \quad ^{-}2 \quad ^{-}1 \quad 0 \quad 1 \quad 2 \quad 3 \quad 4 \quad 5$$

Positive *integers* work like the *counting numbers* and so we do not always use the $^+$ sign.
$\{^+1, ^+2, ^+3, ^+4, ^+5 \ldots\} = \{1, 2, 3, 4, 5 \ldots\}$

See **Integers, Negative numbers**

Power of a number

The power of a number is the result of a multiplication using just that number.

Examples:

$2 \times 2 \times 2 = 8$	8, 32, and 4
$2 \times 2 \times 2 \times 2 \times 2 = 32$	are some
$2 \times 2 = 4$	powers of 2

2 to the power 3 is $2 \times 2 \times 2$ and is written as 2^3
2 to the power 5 is $2 \times 2 \times 2 \times 2 \times 2$ and is written as 2^5

Similarly
$2^{10} = 2 \times 2 \times 2 \times 2 \times 2 \times 2 \times 2 \times 2 \times 2 \times 2 = 1024$
$3^4 = 3 \times 3 \times 3 \times 3 = 81$
$5^3 = 5 \times 5 \times 5 = 125$

NOTE: A number "to the power 2" is said to be *squared*.

7^2 is 7 squared
$\quad = 7 \times 7$
$\quad = 49$

It is equal to the *area* of a *square* of side 7.
See **Exponent**

A number "to the power 3" is said to be *cubed*.
3^3 is 3 cubed
$\quad = 3 \times 3 \times 3$
$\quad = 27$
It is equal to the *volume* of a *cube* of side 3.

Prime factors

Prime factors of a number are *factors* of the number that are also *prime numbers*.

Example:
$\{$factors of 24$\} = \{1, 2, 3, 4, 6, 8, 12, 24 \}$
$\qquad\qquad\qquad\qquad$ prime numbers

$\{$prime factors of 24$\} = \{2, 3\}$

NOTE: We can write any number as a *product* of prime factors.

Examples:

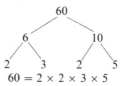

$$18 = 2 \times 3 \times 3 \qquad 60 = 2 \times 2 \times 3 \times 5$$

See **Factoring, Factors**

Prime number

A prime number has only two *factors*, itself and 1.

Examples:
$17 = 17 \times 1 \qquad 13 = 13 \times 1$
17 and 13 cannot be written as *products* of any other *counting numbers*.
{prime numbers} = {2, 3, 5, 7, 11, 13, 17, 19, 23, 29, 31, 37, 41, 43...}
A prime number is a number that is not a *rectangle number*.
NOTE: The number 1 is not a prime number and it is not a rectangle number.

Prism

A prism is a *polyhedron* with the same shape along its length.
Examples:

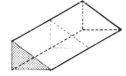 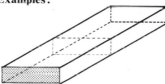 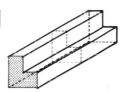

Probability

Probability is a measure of how likely an event is.
The probability of an event is a number between 0 and 1.

Examples:
Probability of a man having two heads is 0.
Probability of rolling a three with one die is $\frac{1}{6}$ or 0.16666...
Probability of a newborn baby being a boy is $\frac{1}{2}$ or 0.5.
Probability of not picking a spade from a new pack of cards is $\frac{3}{4}$.
Probability of your dying in the next 200 years is 1.
Mathematically,
probability of an event S = $\dfrac{\text{number of ways S can happen}}{\text{number of possible outcomes}}$
provided that the possible outcomes are all *equally likely*.

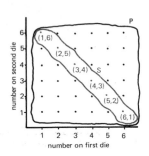

Example (left):
S = {a total score of seven when two dice are rolled}
P = {all possible number pairs when two dice are rolled}
S = {(1, 6), (2, 5), (3, 4), (4, 3), (5, 2), (6, 1)}
number in S is 6
P = {all 36 points on the graph}
number in P is 36.

Therefore, the probability of scoring seven when two dice
are rolled is $\frac{6}{36}$
$= \frac{1}{6}$

Product

The product of two numbers, the multiplier and the multiplicand,
is the result of multiplying them.

Examples:
The product of 6 and 7 is $6 \times 7 = 42$
The product of 2 and 5 is $2 \times 5 = 10$
The same word is used for the result of multiplying two *matrices*.

Proportion

Two quantities are in proportion when corresponding pairs are
always in the same *ratio*.

Example: The number of pens, n, bought in a shop at a cost
of C dollars is shown in this table:

Number of pens, n	1	2	3	4	5	10	20
Cost of pens, C	$2	$4	$6	$8	$10	$20	$40

The ratios 2 to 4, 5 to 10, 20 to 40, etc., are equal, so the
quantities n and C are in proportion.

Pyramid

A pyramid is a *polyhedron* with a *polygon* for a base *face* and all
other *faces* meeting at one *vertex* called the apex.

Examples: The bases are shaded red and some apexes are shown
by a red dot.

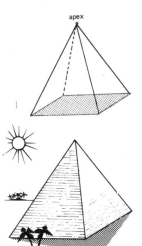

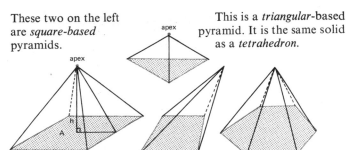

These two on the left are *square-based* pyramids.

This is a *triangular*-based pyramid. It is the same solid as a *tetrahedron*.

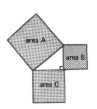

The *volume* of ANY pyramid is given by:

volume = $\frac{1}{3}$ × base area × *perpendicular* height of the apex above the base

$$V = \frac{1}{3}Ah$$

Pythagorean rule

For every right triangle, the sum of the areas of the squares on the legs equals the area of the square on the hypotenuse.

Area A = Area B + Area C

OR

$$p^2 = q^2 + r^2$$

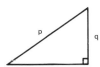

Examples:

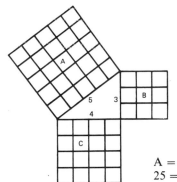

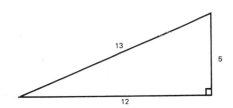

A = B + C
25 = 9 + 16

OR

$5^2 = 3^2 + 4^2$

$13^2 = 12^2 + 5^2$
$169 = 144 + 25$

Some *sets* of three numbers that fit this pattern are

{3, 4, 5}   {5, 12, 13}   {8, 15, 17}
{7, 24, 25}   {20, 21, 29}   {12, 35, 37}

See **Sine**

Quadratic equation

A quadratic equation in x is an *equation* involving x to the *power* 2 but no higher powers of x.
The general form of a quadratic equation is
$ax^2 + bx + c = 0$

Examples:
$x^2 - 2x + 1 = 0$ $x^2 + 1 = 26$ $3x^2 = 12$

When a quadratic equation has *solutions*, and the equation is written in the general form, the solutions can be found using the *formula*

$$x = \frac{-b \pm \sqrt{b^2 - 4ac}}{2a}$$

Quadratic relation

A quadratic relation is a *relation* of the form
$$x \rightarrow ax^2 + bx + c \quad \text{where } a \neq 0$$

Examples:
$x \rightarrow 2x^2$
$x \rightarrow x^2 + 3$
$x \rightarrow 5x^2 + x - 13$
$x \rightarrow 9 - x^2$

Quadrilateral

A quadrilateral is a *plane shape*, or polygon, with four straight sides, and four angles whose sum is 360°.

Examples:

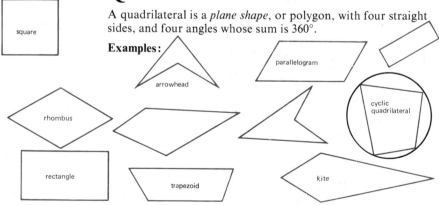

square

arrowhead

parallelogram

cyclic quadrilateral

rhombus

rectangle

trapezoid

kite

Quartile

When there is a large amount of *data*, some idea of its spread is given by the quartiles. These are the values for which $\frac{1}{4}$ or $\frac{1}{2}$ or $\frac{3}{4}$ of the data is less. A *cumulative frequency* diagram may be used to find the quartiles.

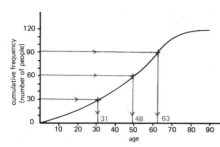

Example (left): In a small village there are 120 people.
The first quartile is up to 31 years old because
$\frac{1}{4}$ of the people are 31 years or less.
The second quartile is 49 years because $\frac{1}{2}$ of the
people are 49 years or less.
The third quartile is 63 years because $\frac{3}{4}$ of the
people are 63 years or less.

Quotient

The quotient is the quantity resulting from the division of a
dividend by a *divisor*.

Example:

In the division $\frac{703}{6)4218}$ 703 is the quotient.

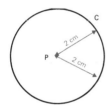

Radius

The radius of a *circle* is the distance from the center of the circle
to a point on the circle.

Example (left):
All the points on the circle C are 2 cm from the center P.

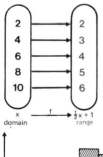

Range

First meaning

(*Mappings*). The range of a *function* is the *set* of numbers onto
which the *domain* is *mapped*. The range is the same as the *image
set*.

Example (left):

{2, 4, 6, 8, 10} is the domain.   {2, 3, 4, 5, 6} is the range.

Second meaning

(Statistics). In a collection of *data*, the range is the *difference*
between the highest and the lowest values.

Example:

135 children took an examination:
the lowest mark was 11 and
the highest mark was 91.
The range is $91 - 11 = 80$ marks.

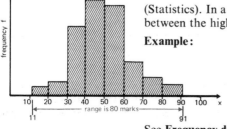

See **Frequency diagram**

Ratio

A ratio is used to compare two or more quantities.

Examples:

A youth club has 30 boy members and 40 girl members.
  The ratio of boys to girls is 30 to 40 (30 : 40).

A football team has won 17 games and lost 10 games.
  The ratio of wins to losses is 17 to 10 (17 : 10).

LEAGUE TABLE		
	Won	Lost
Chelsea	5	11
Newcastle	20	6
Leeds	17	10
West Ham	14	14
Ipswich	12	19

With each ratio we think of a *fraction* that goes with it.

Examples:

The ratio 30 to 40 and the fraction $\frac{30}{40}$ or $\frac{3}{4}$.

The ratio 7 to 3 and the fraction $\frac{7}{3}$.

NOTE: Ratios are equal when their fractions are *equivalent*.

Rational numbers

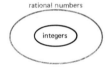

A rational number is one that can be written as a *fraction*.

The *set* of rationals is $\left\{ \frac{p}{q} \right.$ such that p and q are *integers*.

$q \neq 0$, and p and q have no common *factor* $\left. \right\}$.

Examples: $\frac{2}{3}$, $\frac{-7}{8}$, $\frac{15}{19}$, $\frac{8}{1}$, $\frac{1}{13}$, $\frac{-42}{5}$ are examples of rational numbers.

The set of rational numbers is a *subset* of the set of *real numbers*.

The set of integers is a subset of the set of rational numbers.

NOTE: A rational number can always be written as a decimal that either *terminates* or *repeats*.

See **Irrational numbers**

Ray

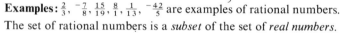

A part of a line that has one endpoint and extends endlessly in one direction.

OP and OR are rays.

Real numbers

The *set* of real numbers is the set of ALL numbers that can be written as a decimal.

The set of real numbers is the *union* of the set of *rational* numbers and the set of *irrational* numbers.

NOTE: An example of a number that is NOT real is $\sqrt{^-1}$. Numbers such as $\sqrt{^-1}$, $\sqrt{^-7}$, and $\sqrt{^-16}$ are called complex numbers.

See **Continuous quantity**

Reciprocal

The reciprocal of a number x is the number $\frac{1}{x}$

Examples:
The reciprocal of 2 is $\frac{1}{2}$.
The reciprocal of 8 is $\frac{1}{8}$.
The reciprocal of $\frac{1}{3}$ is 3.
The reciprocal of $\frac{4}{7}$ is $\frac{7}{4}$.
The reciprocal of $\frac{10}{3}$ is $\frac{3}{10}$.
The reciprocal of a number is the same as the *multiplicative inverse* of the number.

Rectangle

A rectangle is a *quadrilateral* formed by two pairs of *parallel* lines crossing at *right angles*.

Examples:

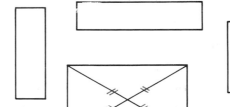

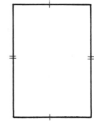

In general a rectangle has:

- two *lines of symmetry*;
- *rotational symmetry* of *order* 2;
- opposite sides equal and *parallel*;
- all four *angles* of the figure equal to 90°;
- *diagonals* equal and *bisecting* each other.

See **Square**

Rectangle number

A rectangle number is a number that can be shown as a pattern of dots in the shape of a *rectangle*.

Examples:

$6 = 2 \times 3$ $16 = 4 \times 4$ or $16 = 2 \times 8$

$21 = 3 \times 7$

{rectangle numbers} = {4, 6, 8, 9, 10, 12, 14, 15, 16, 18, . . .}

See **Prime number** and **Square number**

NOTE: The number 1 is not a rectangle number and it is not a *prime number*.

Rectangular prism

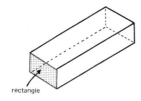
rectangle

A rectangular prism is a *prism* with the shape of a *rectangle* along its length.

Reflection

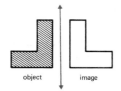
object   image

Reflection is a way of *transforming* a shape as a mirror does. In a *plane*, the result of giving an *object* a reflection in a mirror line is called its mirror *image*.

Example (right):

If P and P′ are *corresponding points*, then the mirror line m is a *mediator* of PP′.

Reflection matrices

Some of the simpler reflections that can be represented as a 2 by 2 *matrix* are

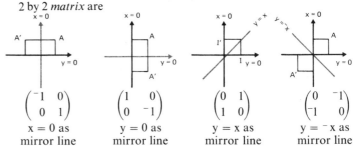

$$\begin{pmatrix} ^-1 & 0 \\ 0 & 1 \end{pmatrix}$$
$x = 0$ as mirror line

$$\begin{pmatrix} 1 & 0 \\ 0 & ^-1 \end{pmatrix}$$
$y = 0$ as mirror line

$$\begin{pmatrix} 0 & 1 \\ 1 & 0 \end{pmatrix}$$
$y = x$ as mirror line

$$\begin{pmatrix} 0 & ^-1 \\ ^-1 & 0 \end{pmatrix}$$
$y = ^-x$ as mirror line

Reflex angle

A reflex angle is an *angle* that is more than 180° and less than 360°.

Examples:

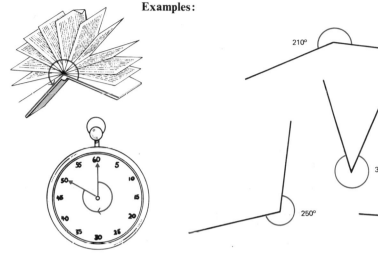

Region

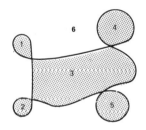

A region is a part of a surface.

Regions in topology

In *topology* a region is a space bounded by *arcs*.

Example (left):

In this *network* there are six regions. Five of the six regions are shaded red, and the space surrounding the network is another region.

See **Euler's formula, Network**

Regions on a graph

On a *graph* a straight line divides the *plane* into two regions.

Examples:

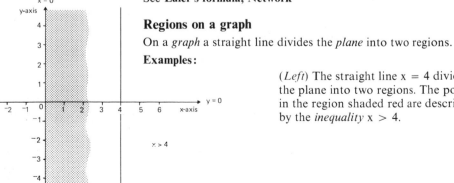

(*Left*) The straight line x = 4 divides the plane into two regions. The points in the region shaded red are described by the *inequality* x > 4.

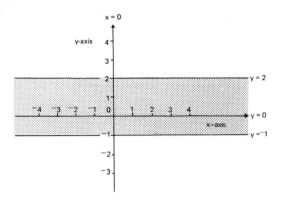

(*Below*) The straight lines y = ⁻1 and y = 2 divide the plane into three regions. The points in the region shaded red are described by the inequality ⁻1 < y < 2.

Regular

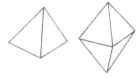

Regular polygon

A regular *polygon* has all its sides the same length and all its *angles* the same size.

Examples (left):

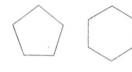

Regular polyhedron

A regular *polyhedron* is a polyhedron with *identical* regular polygons for all of its *faces*.

Relation

A relation is a way of connecting *sets* of things, such as numbers or people.

Examples:

"——is the mother of——"
"——is a factor of——"
"——is 5 more than——"
"——is greater than——"

Relations can be shown by an *arrow diagram* or a *relation diagram*. (There is no real difference between these two.)

Relations which are mappings

A *mapping* is a special relation. See **Mapping.**
Most mathematical relations are mappings and are called either mappings or *functions*. See **Function.**
The same mathematical relation can be shown in various ways.

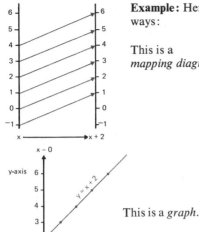

Example: Here is just ONE relation but shown in SIX DIFFERENT ways:

This is a *mapping diagram.*

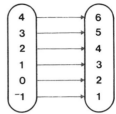

This is a *relation diagram.*

This is a set of *ordered pairs.*

$\{(^-1, 1), (0, 2), (1, 3), (2, 4), (3, 5), (4, 6)\}$

This is a *graph.*

$x \rightarrow x + 2$ This is a relation, or mapping.

$y = x + 2$ This is an *equation.*

Relation diagram

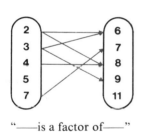

A relation diagram is similar to an *arrow diagram* and is used to show a *relation.*

Example (left):

"——is a factor of——"

Repeating decimal

A repeating decimal has one *digit*, or a group of digits, that is repeated endlessly.

Examples:

$\frac{1}{3} = 0.333333\ldots$ $\frac{6}{11} = 0.545454\ldots$
$\frac{1}{7} = 0.142857142857142857\ldots$

We shorten these answers like this:

$\frac{1}{3} = 0.\dot{3}$ $\frac{6}{11} = 0.\dot{5}\dot{4}$ $\frac{1}{7} = 0.\dot{1}4285\dot{7}$

NOTE: $0.404004000400004000004000004\ldots$
has a kind of repeating pattern but it is NOT a repeating decimal (it is an *irrational number*).

89

Rhombus

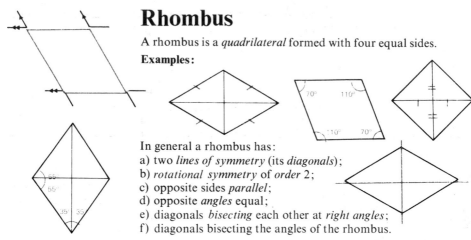

A rhombus is a *quadrilateral* formed with four equal sides.

Examples:

In general a rhombus has:
a) two *lines of symmetry* (its *diagonals*);
b) *rotational symmetry* of *order 2*;
c) opposite sides *parallel*;
d) opposite *angles* equal;
e) diagonals *bisecting* each other at *right angles*;
f) diagonals bisecting the angles of the rhombus.

Right angle

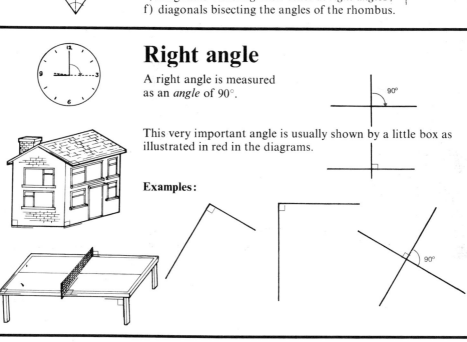

A right angle is measured
as an *angle* of 90°.

This very important angle is usually shown by a little box as
illustrated in red in the diagrams.

Examples:

Right triangle

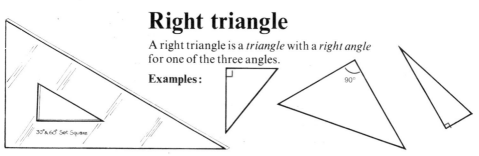

A right triangle is a *triangle* with a *right angle*
for one of the three angles.

Examples:

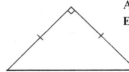

A right *isosceles* triangle has two equal sides and a right angle.

Examples:

See **Pythagorean rule**

Rotation

A rotation is a *transformation* in which every point turns through the same *angle* about the same center. The *center of* the *rotation* is the one point that is *invariant*.

Example (right): In this rotation each line a, b, and c has turned through an angle of 60° about the center O.
A rotation of 60° about O gives the red P as the image of the black P.

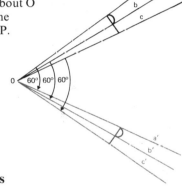

Rotation matrices

Some of the simpler rotations that can be represented as a 2 by 2 *matrix* are those rotations about the *origin*.

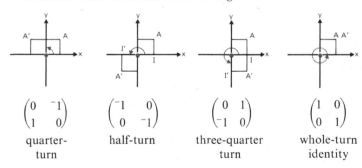

$\begin{pmatrix} 0 & ^-1 \\ 1 & 0 \end{pmatrix}$	$\begin{pmatrix} ^-1 & 0 \\ 0 & ^-1 \end{pmatrix}$	$\begin{pmatrix} 0 & 1 \\ ^-1 & 0 \end{pmatrix}$	$\begin{pmatrix} 1 & 0 \\ 0 & 1 \end{pmatrix}$
quarter-turn	half-turn	three-quarter turn	whole-turn identity

The matrix equivalent to a rotation through an *angle* θ

is $\begin{pmatrix} \cos\theta & -\sin\theta \\ \sin\theta & \cos\theta \end{pmatrix}$

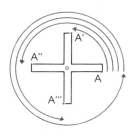

Rotational symmetry

A shape has rotational *symmetry* if, after a *rotation*, every *image* point is *mapped onto* the *object* shape.

Examples: The shape on the left has rotational symmetry. There are four rotations about O, which will map each point of the shape onto itself.

A rotation of 90° about O will map, for example, A onto A'.
A rotation of 180° about O will map, for example, A onto A".
A rotation of 270° about O will map, for example, A onto A'''.
A rotation of 360° about O will map, for example, A onto A.

For this fan, the red line is an *axis* of rotational symmetry. The solid shape can be rotated about the axis through 120°, or 240°, or 360°, mapping each point of a blade onto a point of another blade.

Order of rotational symmetry

The order of rotational symmetry for a shape is the number of possible rotations that give rotational symmetry.

Examples:

For this shape the order of rotational symmetry is 4.

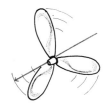

For this fan, the order of rotational symmetry is 3.

order of
rotational
symmetry is 1

order of
rotational
symmetry is 2

Rounding

Rounding a number is a way of writing the number with fewer non-*zero digits*.

Examples:

$1.02 to the nearest dollar is $1.
$17.31 to the nearest dollar is $17.
$.91 to the nearest dollar is $1.
308.5 to the nearest whole number is 309.
0.612 to the nearest whole number is 1.
0.498 to the nearest whole number is 0.
13.77 to the nearest whole number is 14.

When the first digit to be ignored (shown in red) is a 5, 6, 7, 8, or 9 the number is rounded up. When it is a 0, 1, 2, 3, or 4, the number is rounded down.

Examples:

2392 to the nearest hundred is 2400 (rounded up).
2342 to the nearest hundred is 2300 (rounded down).
72,849 to the nearest hundred is 72,800 (rounded down).
106,951 to the nearest hundred is 107,000 (rounded up).
687 to the nearest ten is 690 (rounded up).
9619 to the nearest thousand is 10,000 (rounded up).

Route matrix

In a *network*, a route matrix is a *matrix* showing the number of *arcs* connecting each pair of *nodes*.

Example: For the network below, the route matrix is **M**.

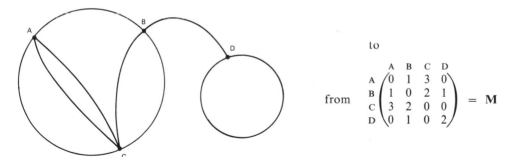

$$
\text{from} \quad
\begin{array}{c}
A \\ B \\ C \\ D
\end{array}
\begin{array}{c}
\text{to} \\
\begin{array}{cccc}
A & B & C & D
\end{array} \\
\begin{pmatrix}
0 & 1 & 3 & 0 \\
1 & 0 & 2 & 1 \\
3 & 2 & 0 & 0 \\
0 & 1 & 0 & 2
\end{pmatrix}
\end{array}
= \mathbf{M}
$$

Route matrix usually means *direct route* matrix.

NOTE: The direct route matrix could also be called the one-stage route matrix. A two-stage route matrix is for routes traveling along two arcs. For the above network the two-stage route matrix can be found by the matrix multiplication **M** × **M.**

See **Incidence matrix**

Row

A list of numbers (or letters) across the page is called a row.
Coordinates are always written in a row.

Examples:
(3, 4),   (1, 9),   (⁻7, ⁻5)

When a *matrix* consists of only a row it is called a row matrix.

Example:
(4 2 8 0 ⁻1)

Scalar

A scalar is a real number, as opposed to a vector.
A scalar has NO DIRECTION. A vector has direction.
A scalar is a real number that describes such quantities as mass, time, and speed (but not velocity, which is speed in a specified direction).

Scale factor

A scale is a ratio that compares the dimensions of a model to the dimensions of an object.
When objects are *similar*, their sizes can be compared by looking at the *ratio* of the lengths of their corresponding parts, e.g., the handles of the saucepans.

Linear scale factor

The linear scale factor is the number of times the length on one object is bigger than the corresponding length on the similar object.

Example: The child's chair is made similar to the adult's chair on a scale 1 to 2.
The scale factor for the child's chair from the adult's is $\frac{1}{2}$.
The scale factor for the adult's chair from the child's is 2.

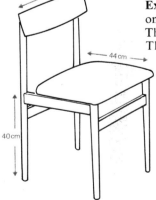

Scale factor of enlargement

In an *enlargement*, a scale factor is used to produce a similar shape.

Example: The enlargement P'Q'R' of shape PQR is made with center O and scale factor 3.

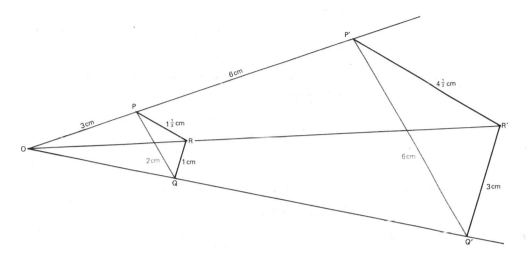

The distance of the *image* point is 3 times the distance of the *corresponding object* point from the center of enlargement:

OP' = 3 × OP   OQ' = 3 × OQ   OR' = 3 × OR

Also, the image lengths are three times the object lengths:

P'Q' = 3 × PQ

Area scale factor

The area scale factor is the number of times the *area* of one shape is bigger than the area of the similar shape.

Example (below):

The area P' is 9 times the area P, so the area scale factor is 9; but the linear scale factor is 3.

If the linear scale factor is k, the area scale factor is k^2.

See **Enlargement** (Enlargement matrix)

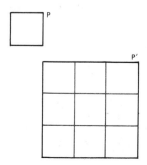

Scalene triangle

A scalene triangle is a *triangle* whose sides are all of different lengths.

Examples:

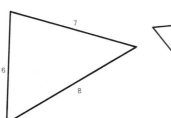

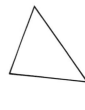

Scientific notation

A number is in scientific notation when it is written as two factors. The first factor is a number between 1 and 10. The second factor is a power of 10 in exponential form.

Examples:

$$400{,}000 = 4 \times 10^5$$
$$9{,}650{,}000 = 9.65 \times 10^6$$
$$1013 = 1.013 \times 10^3$$
$$0.00308 = 3.08 \times 10^{-3}$$
$$7.896 = 7.896 \times 10^0$$
$$= 7.896 \times 1$$
$$= 7.896$$

Sector of a circle

A sector of a *circle* is a shape whose *boundary* is an *arc* of the circle and two *radii* of the circle. It is the shape of the top of a slice of cake or a wedge of cheese.

Examples:

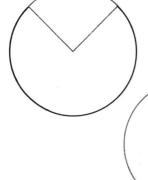

Segment of a circle

The segment of a *circle* is a shape whose *boundary* is an *arc* of the circle and a *chord* of the circle.

Examples:

A chord normally divides a circle into two segments of different sizes. The smaller segment is called the minor segment and the larger segment is called the major segment.

Semicircle

Semicircle means half a *circle*. It is the shape formed by a *diameter* and the *arc* of the circle joining its end points.

Examples:
The *line segment* AB is always a diameter.

A ⎯⎯⎯⎯⎯⎯⎯⎯⎯ B

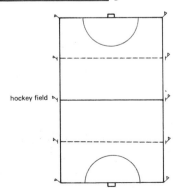

hockey field

basketball court

Sense

Sense refers to one of two opposite directions of point, line, surface, or motion.

If the order of the points A, B, C, D... on a shape is *clockwise*, and the order of the *corresponding points* A', B', C', D'... on a *congruent* shape is *counter-clockwise*, then the two shapes do NOT have the same sense.

Example:

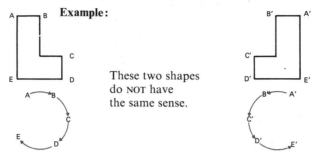

These two shapes do NOT have the same sense.

An *object* and its *image* under a *reflection* (or a *glide reflection*) are always of opposite sense.

When a *transformation* can be represented by a *matrix* **M,** then the *determinant* of **M** shows the sense of the images. If det **M** is *negative*, there is a change in sense; and if det **M** is *positive*, then sense is an *invariant* property for the transformation.

Set

A set is any collection of things. The *members* of a set could be numbers, names, letters, shapes, *matrices*, etc.

Examples:
The set of vowels is {a, e, i, o, u}
The set of *whole numbers* less than 5 is {0, 1, 2, 3, 4}
{*even numbers*} = {2, 4, 6, 8, 10, 12, 14, 16,...}
{traffic-light colors} = {red, yellow, green}

When we use some *elements* of a set A to form a new set, the new set is called a *subset* of A.

Example:
If A = {1, 3, 5, 7, 9} and B = {3, 5, 7}, then
B is a subset of A.

When we put the elements of A and the elements of B into one set, this new set is called the *union* of A and B.

Example:
If A = {t, i, m} and B = {j, i, m}, then {t, i, j, m} is the union of A and B.

NOTE: The order of the elements does not matter, and we never put the same element in a set more than once.

When we take the elements that come in both set A and set B, the new set is called the *intersection* of A and B.

Example:
If A = {△, □, ○} and B = {△, □, +, *}, then {△, □} is the intersection of A and B.

See **Complement of a set, Empty set, Universal set**

Shear

A shear is a *transformation* in which all points slide *parallel* to a fixed line, or *plane*, keeping all straight lines straight.

Examples:

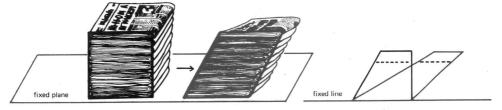

fixed plane   fixed line

The black shape is the *object* and the red shape is the *image* after the shear.

The *areas* of the object shape and the image shape are the same.

Example:
The area of the black triangle is 10 and the area of the red triangle is 10.

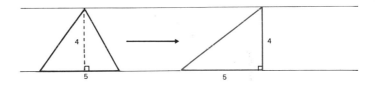

There is always an *invariant* line, and all points move parallel to it. The invariant line need not be on the shape.

Example:
Line p is the invariant line for this shear.

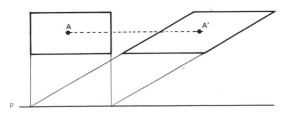

The line joining A and A′, its image, is parallel to p.
The *ratio* of the distance moved by points to their distance from the invariant line is constant.

Shear matrix

The transformation

$$\begin{pmatrix} x \\ y \end{pmatrix} \rightarrow \begin{pmatrix} 1 & 0 \\ k & 1 \end{pmatrix} \begin{pmatrix} x \\ y \end{pmatrix}$$

represents a shear with x = 0 invariant and the point (1, 0) having the image (1, k).

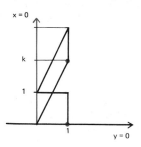

Any *matrix* $\begin{pmatrix} a & b \\ c & d \end{pmatrix}$ where a + d = 2 and ad − bc = 1

will represent a shear.

Significant figures (s. f.)

The most significant figure (or *digit*) in a number is the first digit (not *zero*) that you reach, reading left to right.

Examples:
The significant figures are shown in red.

7861
54002
91
0.006103
0.01007
3.09988

The most significant figures are shown in red.

Shown in red, are:

8140.09   the TWO most significant figures;
61954   the THREE most significant figures;
7089.3   the THREE most significant figures;
60.219   the FOUR most significant figures;
0.042871   the THREE most significant figures;
0.040000   the FOUR most significant figures.

When approximating to a given number of significant figures, *round* the last significant figure.

See **Pi**

Similar

Two objects are similar if they are the same shape.

Examples:

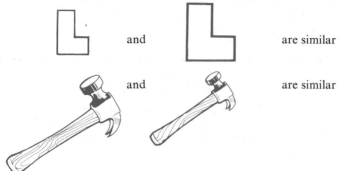

and ... are similar

and ... are similar

With similar objects, all the lengths of one object are a fixed number of times the corresponding lengths of the other object. This number is called the *scale factor*.

Example:

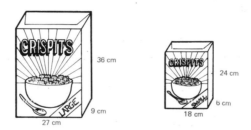

36 cm

9 cm

27 cm

24 cm

6 cm

18 cm

All the lengths on the large box of Crispits are $1\frac{1}{2}$ times the corresponding lengths of the small box of Crispits.

With similar objects, corresponding *angles* are equal.

Example:

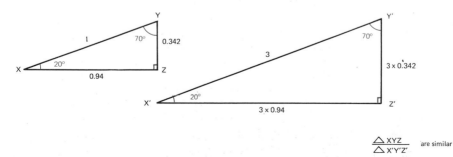

$\dfrac{\triangle XYZ}{\triangle X'Y'Z'}$ are similar

See **Enlargement, Scale factor**

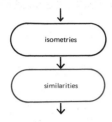

Similarities

Similarities are *transformations* in which *angles* are *invariant*.

Example: *Enlargements* are similarities.

Similarities come after the *isometries* in the hierarchy of transformations. Isometries preserve length, which similarities do not.

Simple closed curve

A closed curve is a line with the end point joined to the beginning.
A simple curve does not have one part crossing another.
A simple closed curve has both these properties.

Examples:

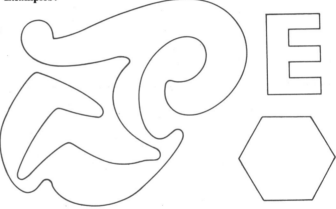

Any *topological transformation* of a *circle* is a simple closed curve. Any simple closed curve can be transformed topologically into a circle.

Simultaneous equations

Simultaneous equations are *equations* that have the same *solution(s)*. The equations are satisfied by the same values of the unknown quantities.

Examples:
y = 2x has many solutions:
$\{\ldots(^-1, ^-2), (0, 0), (1, 2), (2, 4), (3, 6)\ldots\}$
x + y = 3 has many solutions:
$\{\ldots(^-1, 4), (0, 3), (1, 2), (2, 1), (3, 0)\ldots\}$
but if $\left. \begin{array}{l} y = 2x \\ x + y = 3 \end{array} \right\}$ are taken as simultaneous equations there is only one solution, (1, 2) that is x = 1 and y = 2.

If simultaneous equations are shown *graphically*, the solution is given by the *intersection(s)* of the lines.

Examples:

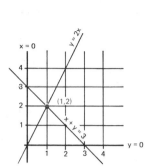

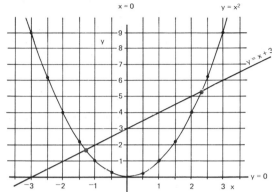

$$\left.\begin{array}{l} y = 2x \\ x + y = 3 \end{array}\right\} \text{ have solution}$$
x = 1 and y = 2

$$\left.\begin{array}{l} y = x^2 \\ y = x + 3 \end{array}\right\} \text{ have solutions}$$
x = 1.3 and y = 1.7
AND
x = 2.3 and y = 5.3

Sine

The sine of an *angle* θ is written as sin θ.

Sine of angles less than 90°

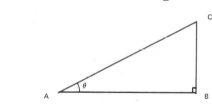

$$\sin \theta = \frac{BC}{AC} \qquad \sin \theta = \frac{\text{opposite side}}{\text{hypotenuse}}$$

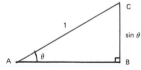

When the length of AC is 1,
sin θ = BC.

When this *triangle* is *enlarged* with *scale factor* r,
QR = r sin θ.

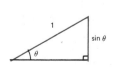

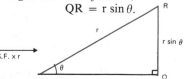

103

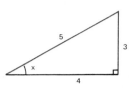

Examples:

$\sin x = \frac{3}{5}$

$\sin x = 0.6$

$\sin 36.9° = 0.600$

$x = 36.9°$

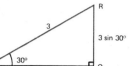

$$QR = 3 \sin 30° \quad (\sin 30° = 0.5 \text{ from}$$
$$= 3 \times 0.5 \qquad\qquad \text{tables})$$
$$= 1.5$$

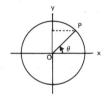

Sine of any angle

If a line OP of unit length turns through an angle θ from the x-*axis*, the sine of θ is the y-*coordinate* of P shown in red.

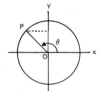 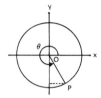

Sine rule

When the lengths of two sides of a *triangle* and an angle (not the one formed by the two sides) are known, then a second angle can be found by the rule

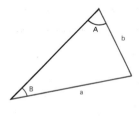

$$\frac{a}{\sin A} = \frac{b}{\sin B}$$

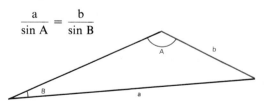

When two angles and the length of one side of a triangle are known, then another side can be found using the same rule.

Slant height

Slant height of a cone

When a *cone* has a *circle* for a base and the *vertex* is above the center of the base, then the cone is a right circular cone. For such a cone, the slant height is the length of a straight line from the vertex to the circle forming the base.

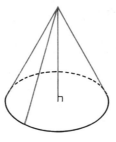

For this cone the slant height is represented by the red lines.

Slant height of a pyramid

When a *pyramid* has a *regular polygon* for a base and the *apex* is above the center of the base, then the pyramid is a regular pyramid. For such a pyramid, the slant height is the length of a line from the apex *perpendicular* to an edge of the base.

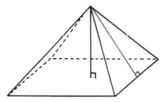

For this pyramid the slant height is represented by the red line.

Solution of an equation

The solution of an *equation* is the *set* of numbers which, when used instead of the letters, make the statement true.

Examples:
$4 + x = 11$ has solution $x = 7$ because $4 + 7 = 11$.
$2 \times x = 10$ has solution $x = 5$ because $2 \times 5 = 10$.
$y - 3 = 5$ has solution $y = 8$ because $8 - 3 = 5$.
$x^2 = 9$ has two solutions $x = 3$ and $x = {}^-3$.
$y = x + 3$ has many solutions; one solution is $x = 2, y = 5$, which can be written using *ordered pairs* as $(2, 5)$.
The *solution set* for $y = x + 3$ with x and y being *integers* is $\{\ldots({}^-1, 2), (0, 3), (1, 4), (2, 5), \ldots\}$.

Solution set

When the *solution of an equation* or *inequality* is more than one number or pair, then the solution is usually called a solution *set*.

Examples:

$x^2 = 4$ has the solution set $\{x = {}^+2, \text{ or } x = {}^-2\}$
or $\{x: \quad x = {}^+2 \text{ or } {}^-2\}$

For x a *counting number*, $2x > 6$ has the solution set
$\{x > 3\}$ or $\{x:x > 3\}$
or $\{4, 5, 6, 7, 8, 9, 10, 11,\ldots\}$

Because a solution set often has many members, it is helpful to show it *graphically*.

Examples:

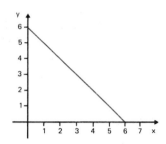

For x and y *real*, $x + y = 6$ has the solution set shown by the red line, that is $\{(x, y): \quad x + y = 6\}$

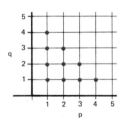

For p and q *integers*, $p + q \leqslant 5, p > 0$ and $q > 0$, has the solution set shown by the red dots, that is
$\{(1, 1), (1, 2), (1, 3), (1, 4), (2, 1), (2, 2), (2, 3), (3, 1), (3, 2), (4, 1)\}$

The solution sets are shown in red:

for x real, and $x > 3$ it is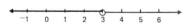

for x an integer and $0 < x \leqslant 4$ it is

for x an integer and $^-1 \leqslant x \leqslant 4$ it is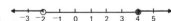

for x real and $^-2 < x \leqslant 4$ it is

Speed

The speed of a body is the distance traveled by the body per unit of time.

Examples:

A car travels along a highway for 2 hours at the same speed and goes 142 *kilometers*. The speed at which the car is traveling is

$$\frac{142 \text{ kilometers}}{2 \text{ hours}} = 71 \text{ kilometers per hour}$$

$$= 71 \text{ km/h}$$

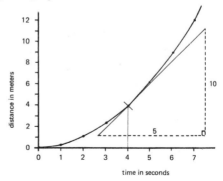

A bullet takes 3 seconds to go 1200 meters. The speed of the bullet changes over the 3 seconds; the "average" speed of the bullet is

$$\frac{1200 \text{ meters}}{3 \text{ seconds}} = 400 \text{ m/s}$$

For a body whose speed is changing, its speed at any instant is represented on a distance-time *graph* by the *gradient* of the curve at that instant.

Example: A marble rolls down a slope. The distance traveled is shown by this graph.

The speed of the marble after 4 seconds is given by the gradient of the red line:

$$\frac{10 \text{ meters}}{5 \text{ seconds}} = 2 \text{ m/s}$$

See **Acceleration, Velocity**

107

Sphere

A sphere is the mathematical name for a perfectly round ball.

Examples:

A soap bubble blown into the air is very nearly a sphere.

The earth and the other planets are roughly spheres.

A sphere is the *set* of points in space that are all the same distance, called the *radius* (r), from a fixed point called the center.

The surface *area* of the sphere is given by:

$A = 4\pi r^2$

The *volume* of the sphere is given by:

$V = \frac{4}{3}\pi r^3$

Square

A square is a *rectangle* with four equal sides.
A square is a *regular quadrilateral*.

Examples:

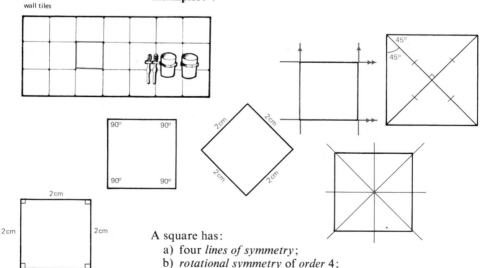

wall tiles

A square has:
  a) four *lines of symmetry*;
  b) *rotational symmetry* of *order* 4;
  c) opposite sides *parallel*;
  d) all four *angles* equal to 90°;
  e) *diagonals* equal and *bisecting* each other at *right angles*.

Square centimeter

A square centimeter is a *unit* for measuring *area* and is equal to the area of a *square* whose sides are one *centimeter* in length. Square centimeter is shortened to cm².

Examples:

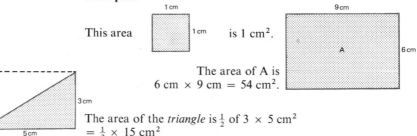

This area is 1 cm².

The area of A is
6 cm × 9 cm = 54 cm².

The area of the *triangle* is $\frac{1}{2}$ of 3 × 5 cm²
= $\frac{1}{2}$ × 15 cm²
= 7.5 cm².

Square meter

A square meter is a *unit* for measuring *area*. One square meter is the same area as a *square* whose sides are one *meter* in length. Square meter is shortened to m².

Examples:

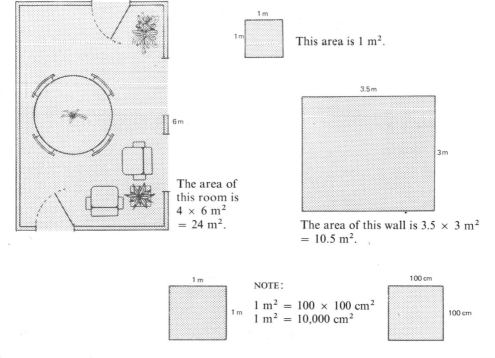

This area is 1 m².

The area of this room is
4 × 6 m²
= 24 m².

The area of this wall is 3.5 × 3 m²
= 10.5 m².

NOTE:
1 m² = 100 × 100 cm²
1 m² = 10,000 cm²

Square number

A square number is a number that can be shown as a pattern of dots in the shape of a *square*.

Examples:

$4 = 2 \times 2$ $16 = 4 \times 4$ $25 = 5 \times 5$

{square numbers} = {1, 4, 9, 16, 25, 36, 49, 64, 81, 100,...}

NOTE: The number 1 is a square number but not a *rectangle number*.

Square of a number

The square of a number is that number multiplied by itself. We often say it is the number squared.

Example: 6 squared is 36.

A number squared means the same as the number to the *power* of 2.

Square root

The square root of a number N can be thought of as the length of a side of a *square* whose *area* is N. It is the number which when *squared* is equal to N.

side of square   area of square
    x   N

x is the square root of N, which is written

$$x = \sqrt{N}$$

Examples:

side   area
 3   9 $3 = \sqrt{9}$

$\sqrt{36} = 6$ $\sqrt{49} = 7$ $\sqrt{1} = 1$ $\sqrt{0.25} = 0.5$

NOTE: The *equation* $x^2 = 4$ has two *solutions* $x = {}^{+}\sqrt{4}$ and $x = {}^{-}\sqrt{4}$

that is,

$x = {}^{+}2$ and $x = {}^{-}2$.

Stretches

One-way stretch

A stretch is a *transformation* in which shapes are pulled or stretched in one direction.

Examples (left):

The red shapes show the *images* of the black shapes after a stretch across the page.

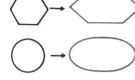

There is an *invariant* line, and all other points move on lines *perpendicular* to this line.

Example:

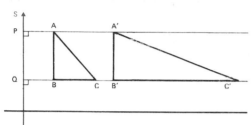

The red line is invariant, and A′B′C′ is the image after a stretch in the direction of the x-*axis*.

Lines PAA′ and QBB′ are perpendicular to the invariant line.

There is a linear *scale factor* k, which gives the amount of stretch. For any point A with line PA perpendicular to the invariant line s, its image A′ is given by

PA′ = k × PA

Example: The invariant line is x = 0. The image after a stretch with scale factor 3 is shown in red.

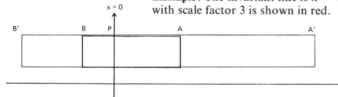

Stretch matrix

The transformation $\begin{pmatrix} x \\ y \end{pmatrix} \to \begin{pmatrix} 1 & 0 \\ 0 & k \end{pmatrix} \begin{pmatrix} x \\ y \end{pmatrix}$ represents a stretch with y = 0 invariant and scale factor k.

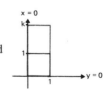

Two-way stretch

A two-way stretch is the single transformation representing stretches with two different invariant lines.

Example:

The image A′B′C′D′ shows the two-way stretch on ABCD:

    x = 0 invariant and scale factor 2,
    y = 0 invariant and scale factor 3.

Subset

If every *element* of *set* B is also an element of the set A, then B is a subset of A.

Example: If A is {a, b, c, d}, then all the possible subsets B of set A are:

{a}   {b}   {c}   {d}   {a, b}   {a, c}   {a, d}
{b, c}   {b, d}   {c, d}   {b, c, d}   {a, c, d}
{a, b, d}   {a, b, c}   {a, b, c, d}   and   { }

When B is a subset of A, we write B ⊂ A.

NOTE: In the example above, all the subsets except { } and {a, b, c, d} are PROPER SUBSETS of A.

Subtend an angle

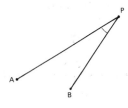

The angle subtended by two points A and B at a point P is the *angle* between the lines AP and BP.

Examples:

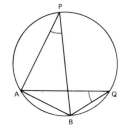

The angle subtended by a *chord* AB of a *circle* at a point P on its *circumference* is equal to the angle it subtends at Q.

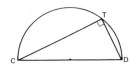

The angle subtended by the end points C and D of a *diameter* of a circle at a point T on its circumference is a *right angle*.

Sum

Sum is the quantity resulting from the addition of two or more addends.

Supplementary angles

If two *angles*, such as 115° and 65°, add up to 180°, they are called supplementary angles.
115° + 65° = 180°.
115° and 65° are supplementary angles.

The opposite angles of a cyclic *quadrilateral* (a quadrilateral in a circle) are always supplementary.

x + y = 180°

Surd

A surd is an *irrational number*.

Examples: $\sqrt{2}$, $\sqrt{3}$, $\sqrt{7} + 1$, $9 - \sqrt{3}$, $\sqrt{8}$, $\sqrt[3]{16}$

Symbols

Mathematical symbols are the signs that are used in mathematics.

Examples:

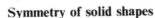

+ − × ÷ ∩ ∪ ∈ ∉
{} = < > Q Z () []

Symmetry

Symmetry is the balance that a shape has.

Symmetry of plane shapes

There are two kinds of symmetry that a *plane shape* can have:

a) *line symmetry*;
This shape has one line of symmetry shown in red;

b) *rotational symmetry*;
This shape has rotational symmetry of *order* three.

Symmetry of solid shapes

There are three kinds of symmetry that a solid can have:

a) *plane symmetry*;
This fish has one plane of symmetry shown in red;

b) *rotational symmetry*;
This propeller has rotational symmetry of order four.

c) *point symmetry*;
This solid has point symmetry.

The full symmetry of a solid is called its *symmetry number*.

Symmetry number

The symmetry number of a solid is the number of ways it can be put into a mold of the shape.

Example:

The red shading shows the four ways in which this solid can be put into a mold. The symmetry number for the rectangular prism is 4.

Tangent of an angle

The tangent of an *angle* θ is written as tan θ.

Tangent of angles less than 90°

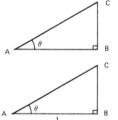

$$\tan \theta = \frac{BC}{AB} \qquad \tan \theta = \frac{\text{opposite side}}{\text{adjacent side}}$$

When the length of AB is 1,
tan θ = BC

When this *triangle* is *enlarged*,
with *scale factor* r, QR = r tan θ

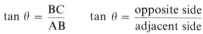

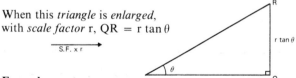

Examples:
tan x = $\frac{3}{4}$
tan x = 0.75
tan 36.9° = 0.751 (from tables)
x = 36.9°

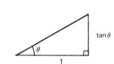

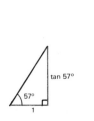

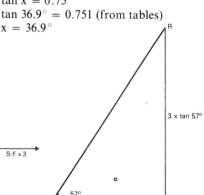

QR = 3 × tan 57°
  = 3 × 1.54
  = 4.62

Tangent of any angle

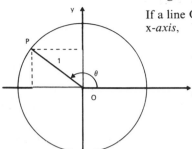

If a line OP of unit length turns through an angle θ from the x-*axis*,

the tangent of θ is the *ratio* $\dfrac{\text{y-coordinate}}{\text{x-coordinate}}$

If P is (x, y),

$$\tan \theta = \frac{y}{x}$$

and $\tan \theta = \dfrac{\sin \theta}{\cos \theta}$.

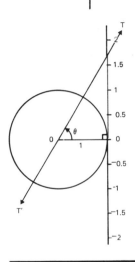

If TOT′ extends without limit in the direction T and in the direction T′, with O the center of a *circle radius* 1, the tangent of an angle θ (formed as the line TOT′ turns as shown) is the intercept made by either end of the line TOT′ with the number line.

The length of the red line is $\tan \theta$.

See **Gradient**

Tangent to a curve

The tangent to a curve is the straight line just touching the curve.

Examples:

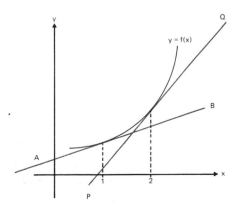

The line AB is the tangent to the curve y = f(x) when x = 1.

The line PQ is the tangent to the curve y = f(x) when x = 2.

Terminating decimal

A *fraction* can be written as a terminating decimal if it can be worked out exactly, without repeating.

Examples:

$$\frac{3}{4} = 0.75 \qquad \frac{7}{16} = 0.4375 \qquad \frac{9}{640} = 0.0140625$$

But $\frac{2}{3} = 0.6666\ldots$ does not terminate, it repeats.

NOTE: A fraction that terminates as a decimal has a *denominator* with only 2 and 5 as *prime factors*.

Tessellation

A tessellation is a way of covering the *plane* with shapes, leaving no gaps and in a repetitive pattern.

Examples:

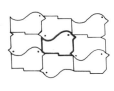

Tetrahedron

A tetrahedron is a solid with four *triangular faces*. It is the same as a triangular-based *pyramid*.

Examples:

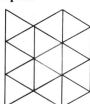

This is a *regular* tetrahedron; all four faces are *equilateral triangles*.

Ton

A metric ton is a *unit* of mass. One metric ton is equal to 1000 *kilograms*. We shorten ton to t.

Example (left): This compact car has a mass of about 1 t.

Topological transformation

See **Topology**

Topologically equivalent

A shape and its *image*, after any *topological transformation*, are said to be topologically equivalent.

Examples: The red images show some possible topological transformations of the black circle. This gives the *set* of topologically equivalent shapes shown below.

Topology

Topology is the study of what happens to a shape if it is drawn on a thin elastic sheet, so that it can be pulled and stretched. It is sometimes called rubber sheet geometry.

Example:

This kind of change is a topological *transformation.* The shape must NOT be torn, and must NOT be joined together, only given twists and stretches (in any direction).

Here are some of the facts that are *invariant* under a topological transformation:

- the number of *nodes*;
- the *order* of each node;
- the number of *arcs*;
- the order of points along each arc;
- the number of *regions*.

In the hierarchy of *transformations*, topological transformations come after the *isometries* and the *similarities*. They allow more distortions, but enough properties are *invariant* for the transformation to be useful.

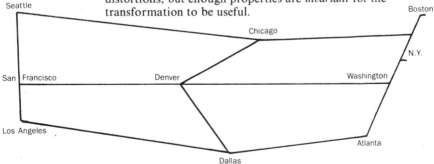

Example: This chart shows relative air distances between major cities in the United States. It is a topological transformation of the actual distances and directions.

Transformation

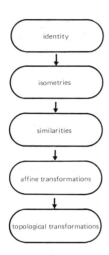

identity

↓

isometries

↓

similarities

↓

affine transformations

↓

topological transformations

When we are *mapping* points and lines, rather than numbers, we use the word transformation.

A transformation describes the *relation* between any point and its *image* point.

The hierarchy of transformations is shown at the left. Under these general headings we find such specific transformations as *rotations*, *reflections*, *translations*, and *enlargements*.

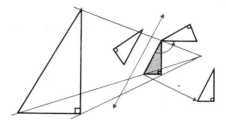

Translation

A translation is a *transformation* in which a shape slides without turning. Every point moves the same distance and the same direction.

Examples:
In each case the red shape
is the *image* after a translation.

A translation can be described by a *vector*.

Examples:

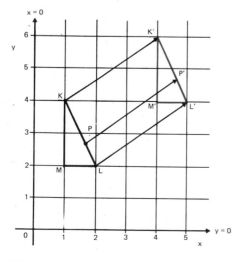

The red triangle shows the image of triangle KLM after a translation

described by the vector $\begin{pmatrix} 3 \\ 2 \end{pmatrix}$

K (1, 4) *maps onto* K'(4, 6)
L (2, 2) is mapped onto L'(5, 4)

by the translation $\begin{pmatrix} 3 \\ 2 \end{pmatrix}$

If P is (x, y), its image P' is found by

$$\begin{pmatrix} x \\ y \end{pmatrix} \rightarrow \begin{pmatrix} x + 3 \\ y + 2 \end{pmatrix}$$

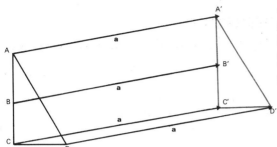

The image A′B′C′D′ is shown in red for a translation of ABCD. Each point has moved the same distance and direction, described by vector **a**. The vector **a** can be represented by red line below.

Transpose

The transpose of a *matrix* **A** is the matrix **A**′ made by changing over the *rows* and *columns*.

Example:

$$\text{If } \mathbf{A} = \begin{pmatrix} 2 & 0 \\ 1 & 2 \\ 1 & 0 \end{pmatrix}, \text{ then } \mathbf{A}' = \begin{pmatrix} 2 & 1 & 1 \\ 0 & 2 & 0 \end{pmatrix}$$

If the matrix **A** represents a *relation*, the matrix **A**′ represents the inverse relation.

Example: For the family, Harry, John, Ian, and Katie, the relation "——is the parent of——" can be shown on an *arrow diagram*, or by means of a matrix.

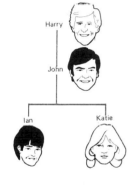

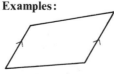

$$\mathbf{P} = \begin{array}{c} \\ H \\ J \\ I \\ K \end{array} \begin{array}{cccc} H & J & I & K \\ \begin{pmatrix} 0 & 1 & 0 & 0 \\ 0 & 0 & 1 & 1 \\ 0 & 0 & 0 & 0 \\ 0 & 0 & 0 & 0 \end{pmatrix} \end{array}$$

The transpose of **P**, **P**′, shows the relation "——is the child of——"

$$\mathbf{P}' = \begin{pmatrix} 0 & 0 & 0 & 0 \\ 1 & 0 & 0 & 0 \\ 0 & 1 & 0 & 0 \\ 0 & 1 & 0 & 0 \end{pmatrix}$$

Trapezoid

A trapezoid is a *quadrilateral* with ONE pair of sides *parallel*.

Examples:

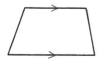

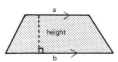

The *area* of a trapezoid with parallel sides of length a and b is given by:

area of trapezoid $= \frac{1}{2}(a + b) \times$ height

Traversable network

A *network* is traversable if it can be drawn without taking the pen off the paper, or going over the same line twice.

Example (left):

The black network is traversable. One possible way of drawing it is shown by the red line.

A network is traversable if either:
a) there are only two odd nodes: (start at one odd node, finish at the other odd node); or
b) there are all even nodes: (start at any point on any *arc*, finish at the starting point).

See **Unicursal curve**

See **Equilateral triangle, Isosceles triangle, Right triangle, and Scalene triangle**

Triangle

A triangle is a *plane shape* made with three straight sides.

Examples:

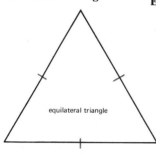

equilateral triangle

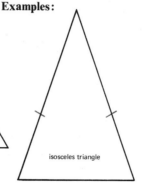

isosceles triangle

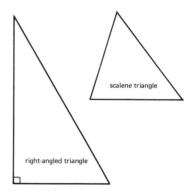

right-angled triangle

scalene triangle

Triangle number

A triangle number is the number that can be shown as a pattern of dots in the shape of a *triangle*.

Examples:

```
                              .
                    .        . .
          .        . .      . . .
.        . .      . . .    . . . .
. .     . . .    . . . .   . . . . .
3        6        10        15
```

{triangle numbers} = {1, 3, 6, 10, 15, 21, 28, 36, 45,...}

NOTE:
$10 = 1 + 2 + 3 + 4$
$21 = 1 + 2 + 3 + 4 + 5 + 6$
$36 = 1 + 2 + 3 + 4 + 5 + 6 + 7 + 8$

Unicursal curve

A unicursal curve is a curve drawn without going over the same *arc* twice, and with the finish joined to the start.

Examples:

NOTE: All unicursal curves are *traversable networks* with even *nodes*.

Only two colors are needed to color the *regions* formed by a unicursal curve. Touching regions must not have the same color.

Union

The union of two *sets* A and B is the set of *elements* that are in A, or in B, or are in both A and B.

Example:

If A = {1, 4, 7, 11, 14}
and B = {2, 4, 10, 14}
then A ∪ B = {1, 2, 4, 7, 10, 11, 14}
The union of sets is shown by the *symbol* ∪

On a *Venn diagram* the union of set A and set B is shown by the set of points shaded red.
A ∪ B is shaded red.

Universal set $\mathscr{E}$

The universal set is the set of ALL *elements* being considered. We use the *symbol* $\mathscr{E}$ to represent the universal set.

Example:

If $\mathscr{E}$ = { *counting numbers* less than 10}
and A = { *prime numbers*}
then A′ = { 1, 4, 6, 8, 9}

On a *Venn diagram (left)* the universal set is shown by a *rectangle*.

Example:

$\mathscr{E}$ = {counting numbers less than 10}
A = {prime numbers}

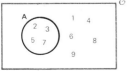

See **Complement of a set**

Variable

When letters such as x and y are used in *formulas* and mathematical *expressions* to stand for numbers, they are called variables.

Examples:
In the formula for the area for a circle, $A = \pi r^2$, r and A are variables, but π is a constant (3.1416...).
In the equation for a straight line, such as $y = 3x + 2$, x and y are variables.

See **Coefficient**

Vector

Vector quantities

Some physical quantities are described by both a size and a direction. These quantities are vector quantities.
Quantities like time, which have no direction, are scalar quantities.

Examples:
Displacement is a vector but distance and length are scalar quantities.
Velocity is a vector because it is speed in a GIVEN DIRECTION.
Speed is a scalar.

A vector is a number store. It is usually shown as a *column* of numbers like this:

$$\begin{pmatrix} 2 \\ -3 \\ 6 \end{pmatrix} \quad \begin{pmatrix} 1 \\ 7 \end{pmatrix} \quad \begin{pmatrix} 0 \\ 4 \\ 18 \\ 0 \\ 1 \end{pmatrix}$$

Each number in the number store means something different. The column of numbers is treated as just ONE number called a vector. We often describe a vector by using a letter. The letter must be either underlined with a "squiggle" like this a̰ or printed in "bold type" like this **a**.

Examples:

$$\mathbf{p} = \begin{pmatrix} 3 \\ 2 \\ -5 \end{pmatrix} \qquad \mathbf{b} = \begin{pmatrix} 1 \\ 0 \end{pmatrix}$$

$2 + a = 5.$
Here a is an ordinary number, known sometimes as a *scalar*, $a = 3.$

$$\begin{pmatrix} 1 \\ 4 \end{pmatrix} + \begin{pmatrix} 2 \\ 3 \end{pmatrix} = \mathbf{a}. \text{ Here } \mathbf{a} \text{ is a vector, } \mathbf{a} = \begin{pmatrix} 3 \\ 7 \end{pmatrix}$$

Vectors as ordered sets

Vectors act like shopping lists, in which the order of the items matter.

Example:

If the vector represents a shopping list for butter, milk, eggs, and bread, each list must show the items in this same order.

2 kg of butter, no milk, 12 eggs, and 1 loaf is $\begin{pmatrix} 2 \\ 0 \\ 12 \\ 1 \end{pmatrix}$

With a friend's list of $\begin{pmatrix} 3 \\ 1 \\ 6 \\ 0 \end{pmatrix}$ the shopping lists together are

$$\begin{pmatrix} 2 \\ 0 \\ 12 \\ 1 \end{pmatrix} + \begin{pmatrix} 3 \\ 1 \\ 6 \\ 0 \end{pmatrix} = \begin{pmatrix} 5 \\ 1 \\ 18 \\ 1 \end{pmatrix}$$

Vectors as displacements

Vectors can be used to describe *journeys*, or *displacements*.

Example:

The journey shown in red is 3 across and 2 up, or as a vector, **d**

$\mathbf{d} = \begin{pmatrix} 3 \\ 2 \end{pmatrix}$.

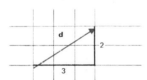

Vectors to describe translations

In a *translation* every point moves the same displacement, so ONE vector will describe the translation.

Example (below):

The black shape is given a translation. The image is shown in red.

For any point P, the displacement P to P' is described by the vector $\mathbf{a} = \begin{pmatrix} 6 \\ 2 \end{pmatrix}$. So this translation is the translation $\begin{pmatrix} 6 \\ 2 \end{pmatrix}$.

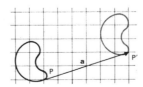

Vector addition

The addition of vector can be performed by adding corresponding items.

$$\begin{pmatrix} a_1 \\ a_2 \\ a_3 \end{pmatrix} + \begin{pmatrix} b_1 \\ b_2 \\ b_3 \end{pmatrix} = \begin{pmatrix} a_1 + b_1 \\ a_2 + b_2 \\ a_3 + b_3 \end{pmatrix}$$

Example:

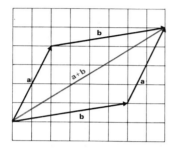

If $\mathbf{a} = \begin{pmatrix} 2 \\ 4 \end{pmatrix}$ and $\mathbf{b} = \begin{pmatrix} 6 \\ 1 \end{pmatrix}$

then $\mathbf{a} + \mathbf{b} = \begin{pmatrix} 2 \\ 4 \end{pmatrix} + \begin{pmatrix} 6 \\ 1 \end{pmatrix}$

$$= \begin{pmatrix} 8 \\ 5 \end{pmatrix}$$

NOTE: The addition of vectors is *commutative*, $\mathbf{a} + \mathbf{b} = \mathbf{b} + \mathbf{a}$,

Scalar multiplying of a vector

When a vector is multiplied by a scalar (an ordinary number) each item in the vector is multiplied by the scalar.

$$k \times \begin{pmatrix} a_1 \\ a_2 \\ a_3 \end{pmatrix} = \begin{pmatrix} ka_1 \\ ka_2 \\ ka_3 \end{pmatrix}$$

Examples:

If $\mathbf{a} = \begin{pmatrix} 2 \\ 1 \\ 7 \end{pmatrix}$, then $3\mathbf{a} = 3\begin{pmatrix} 2 \\ 1 \\ 7 \end{pmatrix} = \begin{pmatrix} 6 \\ 3 \\ 21 \end{pmatrix}$

If $\mathbf{p} = k\mathbf{q}$, where k is a scalar,
then $\mathbf{p}$, shown in red, is k times the length of $\mathbf{q}$ and *parallel* to $\mathbf{q}$.

Velocity

Velocity is a measure of the *speed* with which a body moves in a particular direction. Velocity is a *vector* quantity.

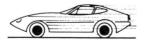

Example: A car whose speed is 40 meter/second has a velocity of 40 meter/second due north if it is traveling in a northerly direction. If the car then proceeds in an easterly direction with the same speed, 40 meter/second, it has a different velocity.

Venn diagram

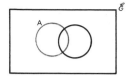

A Venn diagram is used to show *sets*. Each set is represented by the *region* inside a *simple closed curve*, usually a *circle*, and the *universal set* is shown by a *rectangle*.

Example:

Any *element* of set A must be INSIDE the red circle.
Any element not in set A must be OUTSIDE the red circle.

Example:

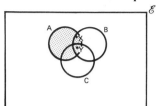

The set A is all the points in the region shaded red.
X and Y are in set A.
X is also in set B.
Y is also in both set B and set C.

Vertex (plural Vertices)

A vertex is a corner of a plane or solid shape. In a *polygon* it is the point where the sides meet.

Examples:

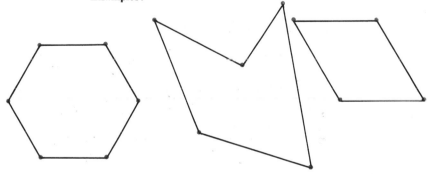

The vertices of these shapes are shown by red dots.

In a *polyhedron* it is the point where the edges meet.

Examples:
All the vertices of this *cube*
are shown by red dots.

A *cone* has only one vertex, which is shown on the cone above by a red dot.

Vertical

A line is vertical if it is *parallel* to a string with a weight hanging on the end. Builders use a weight on the end of a string, a plumb line, to enable them to build walls vertically.

Example (left): The red line shows the vertical line through the string.

Volume

The volume of a solid is the amount of space it occupies.

Example:
The volume of a rectangular prism measuring 3 cm by 4 cm by 5 cm:

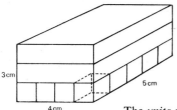

The bottom layer has $4 \times 5 = 20$ cubes.
There are 3 layers.
total number of cubes.
$3 \times 20 = 60$ cubes.
Volume of rectangular prism $= 3 \times 4 \times 5$
$$= 60 \text{ cm}^3$$

The *units* of measurement in the metric system are usually *cubic centimeter* or *cubic meters*.

Volume of prisms

The volume of *prisms*, including the rectangular prism and the *cylinder* is given by:
$V = A \times h$
where A is the *area* of the end and h is the height or length of the prism.

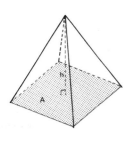

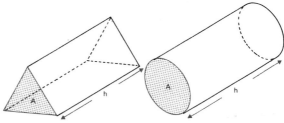

Volume of pyramids

The volume of *pyramids* and also the *cone* is given by:
$V = \frac{1}{3} \times A \times h$
where A is the area of the base and h is the *perpendicular* height.

Whole numbers

The *set* of whole numbers is the set whose *members* are *zero* and the *counting numbers*.

{whole numbers} = { 0, 1, 2, 3, 4, 5, 6, 7, 8,...}

NOTE: The *natural numbers*, or counting numbers, are not usually considered to include zero.

Zero

Zero is shown by the *symbol* 0. Zero has several meanings.

a) Zero is used to show an empty place value in a number with more than one *digit*.

Examples:

2,039 means
2 thousands
NO hundreds
3 tens
9 units

405 means
4 hundreds
NO tens
5 units.

b) Zero is the *identity* for the addition of numbers.

Examples:
$3 + 0 = 3$
$^-4 + 0 = {}^-4$
$0 + 2 = 2$

c) Zero is the point on the number line between the *positive* numbers and the *negative* numbers.

$^-6 \quad ^-5 \quad ^-4 \quad ^-3 \quad ^-2 \quad ^-1 \quad 0 \quad 1 \quad 2 \quad 3 \quad 4 \quad 5 \quad 6$

d) Zero is the number of *elements* in the *empty set*.

$n(\phi) = 0$